CURRICULUM-BASED ASSESSMENT IN SPECIAL EDUCATION

CURRICULUM-BASED ASSESSMENT IN SPECIAL EDUCATION

■

Margaret E. King-Sears, Ph.D.
Johns Hopkins University

With Contributions from
Craig S. Cummings, Ed.D.
Sharon P. Hullihen, M.S.Ed.

Singular Publishing Group, Inc.
4284 41st Street
San Diego, California 92105-1197

©**1994 by Singular Publishing Group, Inc.**

Typeset in 10/12 Century Schoolbook by CFW Graphics
Printed in the United States of America by Bookcrafters

Library of Congress Cataloging-in-Publication Data

King-Sears, Margaret E.
    Curriculum-based assessment in special education / Margaret E.
King-Sears.
        p.   cm.
    Includes bibliographical references and index.
    ISBN 1-56593-099-1
    1. Curriculum-based assessment. 2. Special education. I. Title.
LB3060.32.C74K52   1994
371.2'7 — dc20   93-43364
                                                          CIP

CONTENTS

■

PREFACE

■

One vivid memory about data-based instruction comes by remembering a colleague during the first semester of my doctoral program. He asked if I had used "precision teaching" in my teaching experiences before graduate studies. My instinctive response had been that my teaching colleagues and I had always tried to "teach precisely." But the term posed a perplexing dilemma between what the term meant and how it related to what I knew about teaching and assessment. Fortunately, I was well-schooled in the quantitative methods of teaching, which I've since translated into such educational concepts as "teacher as researcher," "empirical support for effectiveness," "quantitative methodologies," and similar terminologies that can paradoxically enlighten, intimidate, and empower teachers as effective deliverers of instruction.

Curriculum-based assessment (CBA) is an all-encompassing term that can mean most any type of measurement that teachers use. The purpose of this text is to transform the general use of the term into a structured, quantifiable, and useful methodology that can flexibly and effectively be used by teachers of students with mild and moderate disabilities to monitor and improve teaching assessment practices and instruction.

This text can be used in undergraduate and graduate level courses in special education methods or assessment courses. The mnemonic APPLY is used throughout this text as a simple and straightforward method for practicing teachers or preservice teachers to develop and use CBAs.

In this text, you will learn about assessment methods that can be used within all types of general and special education programs. Several qualifying statements are appropriate.

First, don't let the term put you off. You may already be using or approximating the types of data-based instruction described in this book. Preservice teachers will find CBAs especially useful for determining a starting point for instruction. Second, don't let the work put you off. All of the methods described here require a great deal of initial time, thought, and effort — the payoffs *will* come when you plan instruction, involve students, write annual individualized education plans (IEPs) for students, and communicate with other educators and parents about your instructional program.

Finally, be willing to make the changes needed to implement a meaningful assessment that works for you and your students. Continual refinements and revisions of CBAs are necessary when developing practical and relevant assessments for your instructional programs. Educators empower themselves, their programs, and their practices when they develop and validate teaching methodologies and practices within a quantifiable framework. A quality program can always produce quantifiable results — make yours one.

CONTRIBUTORS

■

Craig S. Cummings, Ed.D.
Teacher Trainer, Office of Special Education
Howard County Public School System, Maryland
Faculty Associate, Johns Hopkins University

Sharon P. Hullihen, M.S.Ed.
Coordinator of Learning Center
Montgomery County Public Schools, Maryland
Faculty Associate, Johns Hopkins University

ACKNOWLEDGMENTS

■

Numerous special and general educators and their students have worked with me and contributed many of the ideas and measures you find in this text. I have been inspired and encouraged by their reactions that curriculum-based assessment (CBA) works well for them and their students, and that academic goals are but one of the many benefits of using data-based instruction involving students in their educational program. Many of my colleagues' work samples of probes and graphs are found on the pages in this text. Appreciation is extended to my helpers for their feedback, suggestions, and useful practices in this area. I would especially like to acknowledge the contributions from such master teachers as Teri Musy, Kathleen Chronowski, Gayle Starr, Deborah Fagan, Ellie Giles, and Janet Johnson.

Appreciation is also offered to the personnel at Singular Publishing who have been instrumental in seeing this work through to publication.

Recognition is extended to my husband, Michael, for his understanding and encouragement during this endeavor. I thank him for being my helpmate.

DEDICATION

■

This book is dedicated to my parents, Mary and Joseph King.
Their quantitative union surpasses 50 years;
their qualitative support remains immeasurable.

CHAPTER 1

■

OVERVIEW OF CURRICULUM-BASED ASSESSMENT

■ ADVANCE ORGANIZER ■

This chapter is an overview of standardized testing in special education. Norm-referenced, criterion-referenced, and performance assessments used within special and general education programs are compared to curriculum-based assessments (CBAs). Rationales for using CBA are presented within the broad context of special education programming, with emphasis on how CBAs can be used to write individualized education plan (IEP) objectives, monitor student progress within special education programs, and provide direct links between general and special education programming.

S tandardized tests establish benchmarks of student performance in school curricula. Most standardized tests are characterized by well-established and substantially uniform testing procedures (for example, identical directions are given by each teacher or test administrator) and student output (such as response to test items read silently by the student and indication of answers by choosing from a multiple choice format). Within special education assessment procedures, standardized tests are typically used to assist school committees in making decisions about a student's eligibility for special education services. Assessments for students with mild and moderate disabilities (learning disabled, emotional or behavioral disorders, mild to moderate mental retardation) usually include an intelligence test, achievement tests, and adaptive behavior tests.

Arguments about bias in standardized testings (Galagan, 1985) and content (Salvia & Ysseldyke, 1991) abound, but professionals continue to use these tests because the tools provide a standardized measure useful for comparing student performance to age or grade norms. However, results from these types of traditional assessment instruments are limited in helping make decisions about instructional interventions (Barnett & Macmann, 1992). This predicament is compounded if a student is determined eligible for special education services and an IEP detailing goals and objectives for instructional programming must be written.

For example, consider a sixth grade student who scores at a 3.2 grade level in reading on a standardized test. This information may be useful as a measurement for determining eligibility for special education services for students with learning disabilities, yet the grade level alone does not yield information about specific instructional material that this student requires. The IEP must list the student's present level of performance (which can be interpreted as 3.2 grade level in reading), but the IEP must also list goals and objectives with specific information about what items in reading the student needs to be taught in the next year.

TRADITIONAL ASSESSMENT

Traditional standardized testing is used to differentiate among individuals or groups of students. Standardized tests are typically given to groups of students at specific grade levels throughout their school career. Scores derived from these tests include grade levels (such as the 3.2 reading grade level described above), standard scores, and other types of measures that provide a quantitative value depicting performance of students (as individuals, as groups from the same grade, as third graders' performance within a school district). Norms obtained before widespread administration of a test should be robust and diverse enough to reliably compare one population to another and validly measure important pieces of school curriculum for that grade level.

The most recent update of legislation for special education eligibility (PL 101-476, Individuals with Disabilities Education Act) reiterates previous federal and state regulations that students who are tested and found eligible for special education programming be assessed periodically using appropriate assessment tools. Norm-referenced, standardized tests provide a snapshot of a student's performance within broad curricular areas, but are not sufficient for developing specific instructional plans when educators must write IEPs if a student is found eligible for special education services.

The emergence of more useful and meaningful assessments is occurring — both in general and special education programs (Brandt, 1993; Diez & Moon, 1992; Shinn & Hubbard, 1992). This chapter defines and describes various types of assessments and differentiates how tests are used and implications for decisions made for instructional programming.

Norm-referenced Assessment

Norm-referenced tests are standardized tests initially given to large numbers of students, representing the average student performance (or "norm"), to provide a benchmark for measurement of future groups of students who will take the same test. Norm-referenced test results are typically used to determine how school districts and states are performing in relation to other school districts and states. When school teams (school psychologist, general education teacher, special education teacher, parents, administrator) are making decisions about a student's eligibility for special education programming, an individual student's performance can be compared to local and national students' performance.

Norm-referenced tests generally are questioned on such bases as curricular-match and student characteristic issues. If the content tested does not match the curriculum taught in a particular school district, the validity of the results may be low. Additionally, if the student characteristics included in the population from which the test was initially normed do not match the student characteristics of a given school district, then some educators question whether or not it is fair to compare the two to each other.

Such arguments are enhanced when concerns about lack of a "national curriculum" and useful, meaningful methods of assessing all U.S. students are incorporated. Furthermore, validity (relevance of test content to local curricula) and reliability (dependable, stable test results) issues remain questionable points when results do not appear to be (a) testing what was taught and (b) accurate indicators of student performance. Rather, any score must be interpreted in light of a one-time assessment instead of an ongoing assessment.

Consider that 8,000 3rd, 5th, 8th, and 11th grade students from classrooms representing varied geographic and demographic classrooms in the United States take tests designed for their grade level content to determine what the "normal" students from those grade levels should know. Typically, these are multiple choice tests that yield grade level, stanine, and standard score numbers. The manner in which the test is presented to students (e.g., teacher directions) must be strictly adhered to so that this standard for a classroom in Kentucky is the same as the standard for a classroom in California. Results from such an administration process compose national data of norm-referenced, standardized tests against which future administration of the same test will be compared.

Some norm-referenced tests are standardized based on group (e.g., classroom) administration and others are standardized based on individual administration. The purpose of norm-referenced, standardized tests is to get a numerical account of how a particular student, class, school, or school district compares to other students, classes, schools, or school districts. Remember, these numerical accounts are based on the original 8,000 students who took part in the original "norming" process. The information gained from these tests is primarily used to see how students compare to a typical population. Norm-referenced tests are typically administered to whole classes at specific grade levels throughout the school career (for example, to all 3rd, 5th, 8th, and 11th graders in a school district).

Within the special education placement process, the individually administered tests are used initially when a student is referred to the school committee, and, if the student is placed in special education, these tests may be given on an annual basis and must be used on a triennial basis to determine ongoing eligibility for special education services.

Criterion-referenced Assessment

Criterion-referenced tests determine student performance relative to a predetermined standard or criterion. Criterion-referenced tests typically pose a series of questions or exercises for measuring a skill, knowledge, or aptitude of an individual or a group. For example, if the criterion is that a student can write the correct answers to math problems involving regrouping, then the student is tested for attainment of that competency. Usually behavioral objectives are written for each of a series of criteria, an example of each objective is given to the student, and the student's progress is noted for that particular problem on that particular day.

One behavioral objective that may be assessed using a criterion-referenced test is "given a reading passage written at the 5th grade level, the student will correctly answer three questions about the reading passage." The test item would include the reading passage, and the student usually is asked to select from several answers to indicate the youngster's response.

Information from criterion-referenced tests is primarily used on an infrequent basis to determine student level of performance. Tests are typically given annually or at several points throughout a school year. Although useful instructional levels of performance can be derived from criterion-referenced tests, these assessments are not typically used on an ongoing basis during instruction. Rather, infrequent assessments serve as benchmarks of progress after instruction, not during.

CURRENT TRENDS IN ASSESSMENT

Nationally, improved accountability for students' performance in general and special education has been of increasing concern. High standards of performance and better assessments of performance are being explored in a number of states. Wolf, LeMahieu, and Eresh (1992) report that "a new level of accountability" and efforts to turn "testing into productive tools" compose the wave of the future. These authors lament that "test data is used to rank, rather than improve, schools and to sort, rather than educate, children." New models of assessment are being developed in general education that include open-ended questions, demonstrations, hands-on experiments, and portfolios of student work (Herman, 1992). These models are being investigated as more relevant assessments than traditional norm-referenced tests by tapping into higher levels of thinking and performing — integrating learning and doing within and across content areas. Furthermore, more emphasis is being placed on teaching students to acquire skills, knowledge, and experiences that directly relate to future roles as citizens and consumers in the 21st century community.

Outcome-based Education

Spady (Brandt, 1993, interview) defines outcomes as culminating demonstrations of learning. He distinguishes curriculum content from performances. For example, he suggests that "the student will be able to list the five causes of the Civil War" is not an outcome worth pursuing, but that "identify and explain the fundamental causes and consequences of the Civil War" would be an enabling outcome more meritorious for teaching and learning.

Four principles guide outcomes-based education. The first is clear focus on what schools want students to know when they exit the education system — not just when they exit the semester or the school year. The second principle is expanded opportunity, which means that students are provided multiple opportunities to learn and demonstrate what they know, as well as varied opportunities to be taught in different ways. High expectations is the third principle, and presents a radical shift from the bell curve mentality to an anticipation of all students accomplishing significant, meaningful, and practical learning. The last principle is to design down, as in designing curriculum back from the point you want students to be at the end.

Spady (Brandt, 1993, interview) characterizes curriculum design and assessment within outcomes-based education as more of a "strategic design." He encourages educators to base current teaching and testing on what students will need to do in their future adult lives. Furthermore, he acknowledges that this approach "puts the whole curriculum content structure up for grabs." Spady encourages educators to use the four principles of outcomes-based education to creatively and consistently improve their teaching and testing process.

Performance Assessment

O'Neil (1992) lists several examples of what some states are using as "performance assessments," which represent a shift from standardized paper-and-pencil tests to more substantial methods of evaluating students' thinking skills or their proficiency when synthesizing content or solving problems. Examples include writing an essay, performing a group science experiment, or defending, in writing, how one solved a math problem. Several names have been used to describe performance assessments, including portfolios of a student's best pieces of work. During portfolio assessment, students may be involved in their learning through the requirement that they select their best work products completed during a grading period and conference with the teacher about the quality of their "portfolio." This process requires students to self-evaluate and self-select their work to rationalize why they believe they have selected their best work. Teachers can write narrative reports or assign grades based on a student's growth and improvement throughout a school year.

To be able to do this requires that both teachers and students communicate and understand the learning standards for a given course or content area and requires much thought since it diverges from the current testing methods.

Currently, experimentation and implementation of outcomes-based and performance assessments are occurring in general education in several states (Brandt, 1993; Frazier & Paulson, 1992; O'Neil, 1992). Initial reactions from educators and students have been positive, yet with skepticism about the change from traditional systems of assessment. Educators are moving forward in the development of outcome measures that are practical, useful, and meaningful. These approaches are still relatively new and are viewed by professionals as a progressive means of developing more appropriate assessments for today's students that promote closer links among assessment, curriculum, and instruction (Wiggins, 1989).

CONTROVERSIAL ISSUES

Despite the potential that different forms of assessment can be more meaningful for teachers and students in both general and special education programs, current practice overwhelmingly uses traditional norm-referenced testing when determining student eligibility for special education programming. For years there have been questions about the appropriateness of the tests on which special education placement and program success judgments are made, including bias against minorities, characteristics of students included — or not — in the norm sample, and the value and appropriateness of the information gained from standardized tests (Wang, Walberg, & Reynolds, 1992). Teams of parents, educators, and assessors use the results of standardized tests to determine eligibility for special education programs. Although eligibility criteria vary from state to state (Mercer, King-Sears, & Mercer, 1990), characteristics of students with learning disabilities, mild to moderate mental retardation, and emotional or behavioral disorders are discrepant enough from those of their peers to warrant additional educational services from special education.

The dilemma of qualification for special education services comes when the team that has determined a student eligible for special education services finds that standardized test information was useful for eligibility decisions, but not for instructional planning decisions that must be written in the student's IEP. Given the current discussions of (a) teacher accountability (Englert, Tarrant, & Mariage, 1992; Simpson, Whelan, & Zabel, 1993), (b) overrepresentation of minorities in special education programs (Ortiz & Wilkinson, 1991), (c) growing diversity of students within general education programs (Stainback & Stainback, 1992), (d) student strategy and higher-order thinking skills development (Englert et al., 1992; Young, 1992), and (e) enhancing students' motivation and responsibility for their learning (Giek, 1992), the use of an assessment and monitoring system that can provide *ongoing* documentation of student success and teacher effectiveness is necessary. CBA employing data-based performance of a student within that youth's curriculum has been on the table for more than a decade as one solution to new challenges (Reschly, 1992).

CURRICULUM-BASED ASSESSMENT

CBA has several critical features common to all models. Common CBA principles are that test stimuli be drawn from a student's curricula, repeated testings occur across time, and the assessment information is used to formulate instructional decisions (Tucker, 1985). Furthermore, these data are represented on graphs. The visual representation of student progress enhances teacher decision making, student involvement and motivation, and communication with parents and other personnel.

However, there are varied CBA models which are often used interchangeably in the special education literature. Choices about which model to use can be dependent on the type of decision to be made about a student (Shinn, Rosenfield, & Knutson, 1989). See Table 1–1 for an overall description of terms, definitions, and possible implementation. Distinctions have emerged in recent years between CBA as an overall and flexible model for determining varying levels of student performance and curriculum-based measurement (CBM) as a standardized and long-term model for measuring student growth across a curriculum and measuring effectiveness of teaching methodologies (for reviews, see Fuchs & Deno, 1992; Knutson & Shinn, 1991; Shinn et al., 1989). Because there are strengths in all CBA models, the examples and references found in this text incorporate and integrate the most powerful aspects of all CBA models. Overlaps, as well as differences, are evident in the descriptions found in Table 1–1, and accompanying citations provide further information about each CBA model.

For example, Fuchs and Deno (1992) state that CBM differs from CBA in that CBM focuses on **long-term goals**, versus the CBA focus on a series of **short-term objectives**. In this text, distinctions among varied terms (for example, CBM, data-based instruction, precision teaching) are not differentiated, but distinctions are made in reference to long-term or short-term assessments. **Although differences among models of CBA exist, the purpose of this text is to encourage educators to select from the broad context of frequent and direct data collection systems that enhance instruction and educational decision making.**

Knutson and Shinn (1991) also describe CBA as CBM, and state that CBM must require direct and frequent measures of academic behaviors,

Table 1–1. A sampling of curriculum-based assessment models.

Term and Definition	Example
Precision teaching uses rate of student response, student self-recording, and standard logarithmic charts (Lindsley, 1990).	Students may correct their own spelling assignments, count the number of words spelled (or correct letter sequences) correctly, and graph their own data.
Curriculum-based measurement uses measurement of proficiency on outcomes toward the entire curriculum for that year, and CBM relies on standardized, prescriptive measurement methodology (Fuchs & Deno, 1991).	Spelling words for the current year are randomly selected to represent varied forms for CBM administration, students are given 2-minute assessments on the words during the week, weekly, or every 2 weeks, and student progress on the long-term goal is graphed and monitored.
Curriculum-based assessment uses test stimuli from the student's curriculum and repeated testing across time, and uses the information to make instructional decisions (Tucker, 1985).	Spelling words for a unit of instruction are quizzed periodically during a given unit of instruction, words correct are graphed, and changes in the instructional programming are made according to student progress.
Curriculum-based evaluation uses task analysis of curricula to provide information about the content of instruction (Howell & Morehead, 1987).	Spelling test results are analyzed for patterns of errors that lead to a following series of short-term instructional objectives or to a remediation unit for deficit spelling areas.

view academic deficit as an interaction of student behavior and academic achievement, and use performance data to problem solve. This definition is consistent with other definitions and interpretations of CBA — a data collection procedure that is a direct measure of student progress within a curriculum, with the data serving as a basis for confirmation of adequate and expected progress as well as determination that effective teaching and learning is occurring. The following describes more specifically how CBA is linked to effective instruction, general education performance, and the development and monitoring of IEP goals and objectives.

CBA Link to Effective Instruction

Analyses of what constitutes "good teaching" consistently include references to educators' monitoring of student achievement and performance within the local school curriculum (Christenson, Ysseldyke, & Thurlow, 1989; Simpson et al., 1993). Whether using direct instruction (Gersten, Woodward, & Darch, 1986), strategy instruction (Harris & Pressley, 1991), peer tutoring (Delquadri, Greenwood, Whorton, Carta, & Hall, 1986), co-operative learning (Slavin & Madden, 1989), or other methodologies that have empirical support for effectiveness for students with mild and moderate disabilities, student performance during instruction is a bottom-line indicator of the success of the teaching and learning process.

Furthermore, among the characteristics of effective schools and effective instruction are high achievement expectations and the monitoring of student achievement (Whinnery & Fuchs, 1992). The most frequently cited benchmarks for effective schools include (a) the evaluation of program success that is based on (b) student achievement data (PL 100-297, Hawkins-Stafford Amendments of 1988).

Effective methodologies in monitoring performance is not a new concept to education, and some practitioners are translating business concepts of accountability to the educational field. For example, Audette and Algozzine (1992) use principles of Total Quality Management to illustrate educational goals as a process of continuous improvement. In a Total Quality Education school, continuous and systematic improvement of teaching and learning is cited as a critical concept that is not readily adopted by educators because it (a) may be perceived as a fad, (b) requires interpretation and training, and (c) challenges the status quo of conducting business in the schools. This book views the use of CBA as a means of continuous and systematic improvement for teaching and learning. Training for and application in the schools must be planned and provided, so educators can assume ownership and responsibility for their data.

Ortiz and Wilkinson (1991) further illustrate the use of CBA as an essential aspect of attaining a nonbiased assessment of students who use English as a second language. The researchers suggest that CBAs examine student performance in both English and a native language, and these assessment results can indicate whether the student's deficit areas are related to their language background or to a disability.

CBA Link to General Education

Idol (1989) refers to CBA as a critical tool for resource/consulting teachers. Special education teachers must be skilled in using CBA to identify learning problems, monitor the effects of intervention, and determine when students are performing at the same level as their age-appropriate peers.

Furthermore, Vergason and Anderegg (1991) identify CBA as an effective monitoring practice that has been widely replicated in special education, and they recommend that CBA be used for improving the outcomes for students in special *and* general education. Students are less likely to stagnate in their educational program if teachers use CBA to oversee that all students make progress.

CBA Link to IEP Goals and Objectives

The link between CBA and objectives listed on a student's IEP is a prime area of concern. Presently, special education teachers spend much of their instructional time at the end of the school year collecting data and writing IEP goals and objectives. When CBA procedures are used throughout the school year, general education standards and educators (including academic, social, and vocational areas) are involved, the student has monitored progress through CBA graphs, and parents have received reports on their child's achievements using CBA, more responsibility can be shared and mutual ownership of progress can be communicated during annual IEP meetings.

Notari and Drinkwater (1991) compare between the quality of IEP goals and objectives written when selecting from a computerized listing and from those written directly from a CBA. Goals and objectives were rated on five criteria: (a) the practicality and usefulness of targeted skills; (b) the generality of the skill being adapted, modified, and generalized; (c) how easily the skill could be delivered within the instructional context; (d) how measurable the skills were; and (e) the hierarchical relationship between the long-term goal and the short-term objective on the IEP. The results of this study indicate that the IEP goals and objectives derived from CBA received significantly higher ratings than those written using the computerized listing of goals and objectives.

CBA's Validity and Reliability

Shinn and Hubbard (1992) emphasize the assessment need for content validity, an adequate quantity of items selected from the curriculum for evaluation, and response requirements that require student productions — which can be analyzed to determine error patterns. Content validity means that "test" items be drawn from the relevant environmental demands, that is, what the student is expected to do within the general education context. An adequate quantity of items selected ensures that a single session or a single item not be the basis for decision making. Rather, information for decisions is based on (a) more than one testing session and (b) more than one item. Such selection also strengthens the reliability of the information gained from the assessment. A standardized assessment format (for example, for directions or how responses are elicited) as well as consistent scoring of items can help ensure reliable results. Finally, analyzing the types of errors a student makes provides specific information about where to begin *and* how to continue instruction.

How CBAs are developed and used is determined by the teacher, and this text guides teachers through several CBA models, while providing the latitude necessary for individual adaptation. However, teachers should standardize the content, items, and conditions of using CBA such that a chosen variable use will not degrade the integrity and influence of reliability and validity.

CBA Uses

The rationale for using any type of assessment must first be clarified. There are several points at which CBA can be used as an additional tool in making decisions about a student's progress and performance. The first is when a general education teacher has concerns about a student and wants to compare that student to other students in the classroom before referring a student for possible special education placement. Data about how a student compares to the classroom norm is useful in determining the discrepancy between students in a particular classroom, grade level, or school district. Furthermore, teachers can experiment with different academic and behavior management techniques to determine if modifications can alleviate initial concerns. Several states already encourage schools to use CBA as an additional measurement tool before referral (e.g., prereferral) to special education and during an assessment process including norm-referenced assessments (Mercer et al., 1990).

Next, if a student is found eligible for special education services, the information gathered from initial CBAs is directly related to the specific instructional goals and objectives written on the student's IEP (see Table 1-2 for a comparison of assessment result language).

Finally, when CBA is used within both special education and general education programs to determine individual student progress and performance, the decision that a student no longer requires special education services designated on the IEP is supported by authentic and practical data that can ensure a timely and appropriate dismissal from special education.

Advantages of CBA include the direct match between assessment items and the tasks, skills, and performance required in the classroom. The teacher has full control over the development and utilization of CBA,

Table 1–2. Example of the detailed results from norm-referenced, criterion-referenced, and curriculum-based assessment.

Norm-Referenced	Criterion-Referenced	Curriculum-Based
Student scores 4.3 grade level in math.	Student computes whole numbers with regrouping.	Student writes correct answers to 4-digit addition and subtraction, with regrouping at a rate of 85 correct digits per minute.

in that flexible revisions and refinements can be easily made. CBA procedures can be employed across content areas. The use of repeated measurements of student performance ensures reliability of results; a one-time measurement session does not. Additionally, the direct match of CBA to the curriculum can ensure curriculum validity; what is taught is what is measured (Deno, 1985). Student maintenance and generalization of skills and strategies also can be monitored through the use of CBA (Ellis, Lenz, & Sabornie, 1987; Fuchs & Deno, 1991).

SUMMARY

One goal when students are placed in special education is that they return to less restrictive environments (i.e., general education classrooms) in a timely and appropriate manner. Another goal is that the content and challenges in special education programs should be consistently and systematically based on what is expected in general education classrooms (Putnam, 1992) or other targeted environments (work setting, community). If the premise of special education placement is that a student has not been successful in general education classes, then the services delivered from special educators need to be those to prepare a student for that success in conjunction with general education (Deshler & Schumaker, 1986). A final goal is that students with mild and moderate disabilities become involved, responsible, and active participants in their educational programming (Mehring & Colson, 1990).

CBA provides data that expedite decision making on the effectiveness of IEPs. There are many validated teaching methods that can be used to ensure appropriate programming and instruction for students with mild and moderate disabilities (Christenson et al., 1989; Elksnin, 1989;

Ellis & Lenz, 1987; Epstein & Cullinan, 1987; Scruggs & Mastropieri, 1992). Data from CBA support the effectiveness of these methods and provide teachers and students with information that should be used in instructional programming.

Chapter 2 describes the APPLY framework and provides other practical suggestions to assist teachers in getting started with CBA, as well as ways to involve students in their educational program by using CBA. Additionally, teachers are introduced to the USEFUL framework, which represents criteria against which teachers can determine how functional, valuable, and practical their individualized CBA is. The remaining chapters in this text use the APPLY framework to illustrate multiple examples of CBA. Furthermore, references and resources for alternative teaching methods are listed in each chapter so that the educator can select from validated methodologies when CBA data indicate that a teaching change is needed.

CHAPTER 2

■

GETTING STARTED WITH CURRICULUM-BASED ASSESSMENT

■ ADVANCE ORGANIZER ■

The APPLY framework for developing and using curriculum-based assessment (CBA) is described, with particular attention to details and decisions that enhance the usefulness of this process. Determining goals and objectives, enlisting student involvement, and using available resources, including computer technology, to increase teacher efficiency and effectiveness are defined as part of the CBA process. Additionally, the USEFULness framework is presented as a guide for teachers in evaluating their CBA. This chapter is a foundation for subsequent chapters focusing on individual content areas.

W hen teachers begin incorporating CBA into their instructional programs, much time is devoted to learning about the process, deciding which skills and content areas to focus on, and determining how to most effectively and efficiently continue using CBA. Although there are many benefits in using CBA (Giek, 1992; King-Sears, Richardson, & Ray, 1992), the initial investment of work and time can be foreboding. Time management techniques and timesavers are provided in this chapter, along with the recommendation that teachers start small with more manageable and succinct CBAs until they have a few systems in place. Once teachers and students are familiar with CBA, it is easier to expand, revise, and incorporate more curricula and procedures to attain higher levels of content knowledge and process.

The term CBA can be defined in several different ways (for reviews, see Fuchs & Deno, 1992; Knutson & Shinn, 1991; Shinn et al., 1989). Some researchers refer to CBA as any method that uses a curriculum to determine student progress. Others tend to use the term as a starting point for instruction versus an ongoing measurement system. Still another distinction is the use of CBA (typically called CBM when used this way) as a measure of long-term goals versus short-term, or subskill, areas. Rather than differentiating among the varied uses of the term, this text presents the APPLY and USEFUL frameworks for combining practical and powerful influences of all interpretations of CBA.

Before beginning to use CBA, teachers must understand the difference between their present data collection methodologies (that is, how they give grades and determine student progress before, during, and after instruction) and the use of a systematic, direct measurement system such as CBA. For example, Cooke, Heward, Test, Spooner, and Courson (1991) found that special education teachers frequently used informal observation to determine if their students had accomplished IEP objectives. Although most teachers acknowledged that data collection was important, the amount of time it takes to collect and graph data seemed to have been prohibitive for the studied teachers. Furthermore, this study reveals that teachers did not appear to be taking advantage of some material (e.g., computer software) and personnel (e.g., instructional assistants) resources generally available to promote and enhance the CBA use. Given the overwhelming literature and research base repeatedly calling for measurement methods such as CBA, it is imperative that teacher trainers and staff development programs consider including additional methods for emphasizing the use of CBA in special education preservice and inservice programs.

The APPLY framework presented throughout this text is also accompanied by suggestions for timesavers that can alleviate some of the initial work that goes into setting up CBA in any classroom as well as its ongoing use. The advice is to get started somewhere in your curriculum with a small group of students — then build on that program and expand into other curricular areas. The payoffs should be rather immediate for both the teacher and the student, but the initial work must be done by the teacher.

APPLY AS A FRAMEWORK

Proponents of CBA have described these procedures in as few as four and as many as eleven steps (Blankenship, 1985; Salvia & Hughes, 1990). The details and sequences described in these steps usually begin with curriculum needs and end with use of the data. APPLY has been developed as a mnemonic to synthesize the steps involved in developing and using CBA (see Table 2-1). Teachers in schools and student teaching settings have used APPLY, and some have adapted the mnemonic with individual steps for themselves, with others developing a personalized process. Throughout this text, APPLY describes CBA in content areas, but educators are encouraged to adapt as might be needed for themselves as a means of ownership and relevancy of the process to help in actual use of CBA.

1. Analyze the curriculum.

Whether a curriculum designed for a student with mild or moderate disabilities includes social skills or vocational or academic content, the development of CBA begins with the curriculum analysis. Awareness of the scope and sequence of needed content guides the educator in determining the critical areas to serve as benchmarks of a student's progress. If success in the general education curriculum is the goal, then collaboration with general education teachers areas is necessary. If success in the work environment is the goal, then collaboration with employers is

Table 2-1. APPLY as a framework for developing and using CBA.

1. *A* **NALYZE** the curriculum.
2. *P* **REPARE** items to match curriculum objectives.
3. *P* **ROBE** frequently.
4. *L* **OAD** data using a graph format.
5. *Y* **IELD** to results — revisions and decisions.

necessary. Additional collaborators may be the speech-language pathologist, counselor, or other school personnel involved in the student's educational program.

Teachers beginning the CBA process need to target short- or long-term objectives for monitoring student progress. For example, if the unit of instruction is on comprehension of reading passages, then the short-term instructional objectives may be vocabulary identification and comprehension from only one or several of the reading passages. Short-term objectives may include those targeted for a unit of instruction or single skills within a unit of instruction or a grading period. However, long-term objectives could include vocabulary and a range of questions selected from reading passages to be taught during that year. Long-term objectives can encompass the short-term objectives, but may be more broad.

Sources for objectives for individual curricular areas may be available from the school district, the IEP, instructional materials (e.g., textbooks), and a student's previous performance in a content area. Curriculum analysis including priorities for that student is essential before moving further in the CBA process. That is, the teacher must have a clear perspective of the instructional objectives, then must decide if short- or long-term measures (or a combination) will be constructed to measure the student's progress on those objectives.

The curriculum needs to be seen as having many objectives, with only a few serving as benchmarks for student progress. Teachers developing CBAs need to determine which of those objectives are the critical benchmarks; thus the teacher can consider individual characteristics of students in developing the CBA. This does not mean that completely different and varied CBAs need to be developed for each student. Rather, once the process of using CBA becomes efficient, teachers are able to use the same CBA for different students, and most individuality occurs based on *how* the data from CBA are used to influence that student's instructional program.

2. Prepare items to match curriculum objectives.

Following determination of short- or long-term objectives, preparing items that match these objectives should be carefully thought through. Because one characteristic of using CBA is that direct and frequent measure of objectives occur, the idea of using small amounts of time (e.g., 1-minute timings for reading vocabulary words) across time (e.g., 3 times a week) should be considered when preparing the items.

Different forms for measuring the same objectives may also be a consideration. For example, a long-term objective spanning a grading period would be that students compute fractions using mixed numbers and unlike denominators. For that example, the CBA objective may formally read, "Given a worksheet of fraction computations that include addition and subtraction of mixed numbers with like and unlike denominators, the student will write the correct answers at a rate of 12 problems per minute." The computations are the items for the CBA. Alternate forms of the same CBA contain different computations that still match those described in the objective. The fraction computations matching the objectives constitute the probing (that is, investigating for information) for student response. That is, the problems become the "probe" for student performance.

Another consideration in preparing items that match a curriculum objective is inclusion of both basic facts and higher level thinking skills. The above example does not measure success with solving word problems, so the inclusion of a word problem or several word problems on the same probe would expand the CBA to cover two objectives — one dealing with basic fact computation and the other dealing with problem solving.

Randomizing the selection of items that will become the probes for student performance, especially when the objective(s) cover(s) a range of skills, ensures greater CBA reliability.

If an objective deals with performing a task in a specific sequence (e.g., changing the oil in a car), then the items prepared for that probe may be a checklist of the steps to be followed.

All items must (a) match the behavior and conditions stated in the objective, (b) be directly measurable, (c) link student performance to curriculum objectives, and (d) be considered as overall indicators of critical performance necessary for students within a given curriculum. Furthermore, it is possible to assess students' thinking processes or strategies for solving problems by requiring verbal or written responses to "How did you get that answer?"

3. **Probe** frequently.

Most teachers consider end-of-week or end-of-unit or end-of-chapter assessments to be frequent assessments. The use of CBA may include such testing, and certainly should be a measure that is directly related to scheduled assessment. However, CBAs are not necessarily used to determine a grade and should be used more frequently within long grading periods. The variation of the frequency with which a teacher probes, or measures, student progress and performance will vary, but needs to be planned carefully so that the process becomes an integral part of the instructional program.

The time spent in CBA testing is cumulative. That is, the total time to be spent in assessment is divided into small intervals, so that a sampling (or, in CBA terms — a probe) of how students are doing with some critical information (taken from behavioral objectives on the IEP) is available during instruction. Teachers can develop a schedule for short probes, usually 1 to 3 minutes. Such probes can be administered as quizzes at the beginning or end of class periods, several days a week (if possible) so that (a) a short amount of time is spent probing, and (b) information gathered between pre- and posttesting lets the teacher know how students are progressing.

For example, a 1-minute probe of math computations may be planned for 3 times a week. The whole process should take no more than 2 minutes to complete. If students correct their probes, graph results, and set goals for their next performance, then more time must be planned for. However, it is critical that teachers ensure that the probes actually yield (a) more student ownership of their work, (b) higher and faster achievement for students by directly involving them in their performance during the instructional phase, not after the test has occurred, and (c) more efficient and effective use of time on-task for students and instructional time for teachers. Some recommendations for 1- to 3-minute timed probes are listed in Table 2–2 for basic content areas.

4. Load data using a graph format.

Information from CBA results in a numerical indicator that is then transferred to a graph. The visual display of student performance can by itself lead to greater achievement (Fuchs & Fuchs, 1986). When students are able to actually see their academic learning result in an upward line on a graph, more motivation and responsibility for learning results. This in and of itself is powerful rationale for the use of graphs. Another advantage is that graphing elicits student involvement in their progress. Other motivational aspects of graphing are discussed later in this chapter.

The graph itself can be developed using basic graph paper. Equal interval graph paper displays identical increments between all numerical indicators; whereas logarithmic graphs show proportional increments between numerical indicators on the graph vertical edge. For example, an equal interval paper would display the difference in the same time period between 10 and 20 as the same difference in the same time interval between 50 and 60. A logarithmic graph would show these differences within time frames as proportional: the distance between 10 and 20 is a times two difference, and the distance between all other vertical numbers would be a "times two" difference in space as well (see Figure 2–1A, B, and C for an example of each graph). For several years there

Table 2-2. Examples of CBA.

Content Area	Time	Description of CBA
Reading	1 minute	The probes are reading passages, which may be selected from any content area. The student reads aloud for 1 minute. Conduct CBA two times per week with each individual. Graph the number of words read correctly and incorrectly.
Math	2 minutes	The probe is a worksheet of math computations. The student solves as many problems as possible in 2 minutes. Conduct CBA three times per week using group administration. Graph the number of digits computed correctly and incorrectly.
Spelling	2 minutes	The probe is an oral or audiotaped dictation of spelling words. The student writes the words. Conduct CBA four times per week using group administration. Graph the number of correct letter sequences or the number of words spelled correctly or incorrectly.
Written Language	3 minutes	The probe is a story opener, which may be a topic or brief story starter situation. The student elaborates on the story opener by writing for 3 minutes. Conduct CBA one time per week using group administration. Graph the total number of words written, number of words spelled correctly, or other salient aspects.

Source: Adapted from Germann and Tindal, 1985; and Shinn and Tilly, 1989.

were discussions among researchers as to which graphic display most accurately (a) depicted student performance and (b) lent itself to more valid instructional decisions and predictions about student performance. Fuchs and Fuchs (1986) say that neither type of graph is significantly superior. Thus, equal interval graphs are used throughout this

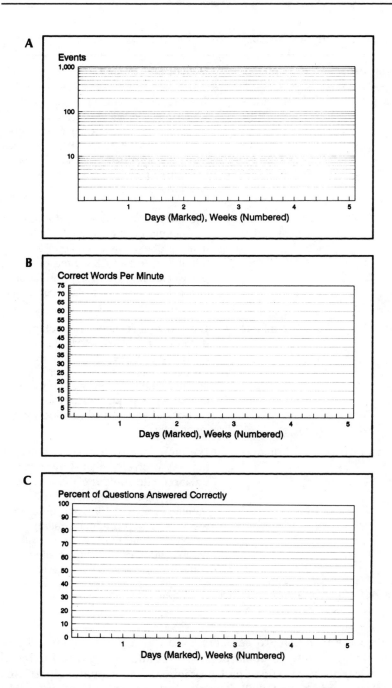

Figure 2-1. A. Logarithmic graph. **B.** Equal interval graph. **C.** Equal interval percentage graph.

text in discussion and examples, because these are more readily available; they facilitate communication with parents, students, and other educators; and logarithmic graph are not significantly superior.

A basic graph format includes labeling the vertical side with numbers along with a phrase that describes those numbers, labeling the dates on the horizontal graph axis, and a title for the behavioral objective that is being measured. Other information may be as basic as the student's name, grade, subject area, or objectives depicted on the CBA graph.

The vertical part of a graph has a sequence of numbers matching the criteria designated in the curriculum objective. If the objective's criterion statement is "10 out of 10 problems completed correctly," then the vertical side should be numbered 1 to 10 and should read "number of problems completed correctly."

The horizontal part of the graph indicates dates or sessions when data were gathered. A recommendation is to use only dates during which CBA was administered. Connect the data points to easily illustrate the flow of performance. Use symbols to indicate different areas of data (e.g., number correct, number of errors), if plotted on the same graph. Color may be added to these symbols, but the visual display of color will not copy if a photocopy of the graph is part of a student's IEP folder or for other dissemination (for example, sending a copy home to parents).

5. Yield to results — revisions and decisions.

The results on a graph must lead somewhere for the teacher and the students; otherwise, those data are worthless and the time spent on the project has been wasted. The data may indicate needed revisions in instructional programs if sufficient progress has not occurred, decision guides on other instructional programs to use, or as documentation of the success of the program. Decision rules and procedures are described later in this chapter (see "Evaluating Performance"). Examples of yielding to student results are also presented in case studies throughout this text.

In some cases, a teacher may return to the curriculum guide, the behavioral objective, and the probe (the AP of APPLY) and revise these elements into more accurate measurement objectives and materials. Such refinements of the CBA process indicate that the teacher is making decisions based on data.

Linking CBA to Individualized Education Plans

The goals and objectives on a student's IEP contain information derived from standardized test results. However, the standardized test results often do not lend themselves easily to instructional objectives. A student's score at the 25th percentile on a test of reading comprehension only tells one where the student falls when compared to the norm group — not instructional information about reading skills to list as goals and objectives on the IEP. In other words, the results of standardized tests often do not lead to specific skill levels or instructional needs.

One solution is to conduct an error analysis of the items missed on a standardized test. This may provide a starting point, but not an ongoing assessment system.

Another solution for the mismatch between standardized test results and instructional information is to develop CBA that sample the behaviors assessed on achievement tests. For example, knowing that a student tested at the 3.7 grade level for computations on the KeyMath test does not yield instructional recommendations. However, a teacher who uses 1-minute CBAs of computational skills (e.g., subtraction with regrouping) is able to target that the student's instructional objective should include acquisition of subtraction with regrouping in the tens and hundreds, and also focus on fluency-building activities (e.g., basic subtraction facts).

A student's IEP lists goals and objectives that comprise the major areas for CBA. Some IEP goals may be as vague as "increase reading vocabulary" or as explicit as "increase recognition of Dolch sight words from 20 words to 200 words from the Dolch sight word list using direct instruction teaching procedures." With the long-term goal usually stated for 1 year, the objectives on IEPs state short-term steps that lead to that goal. Expanding on the above goal, the short-term objective may be "When given a listing of 40 Dolch words, the student will verbally identify the words correctly." Exemplary IEPs contain such behavioral objectives that can be used as written to develop CBAs.

Developing Behavioral Objectives

Behavioral objectives contain a verb that clearly states the behavior that will be observed, conditions under which the student will be assessed, and the degree or criterion against which mastery of the objective can be measured. Behavioral objectives should be written that encompass low- and high-order thinking skills, such as those depicted on Bloom's taxonomy (see Table 2–3) of cognition (Mager, 1962; Rosenshine & Meister, 1992). Additionally, the condition statement for some IEP objectives should include the generalization environments (e.g., general education classroom, work setting). Haring and Liberty (1990) emphasize that programming for generalization is often necessary to ensure that students transfer skills and strategies learned in special

Table 2-3. Bloom's taxonomy and verbs for behavioral objectives.

Bloom's Hierarchy of Cognition		Examples of Verbs
Knowledge	↓	list, recall, name
Comprehension	↓	describe, explain, negotiate
Application	↓	solve, demonstrate, interpret
Analysis	↓	compare, distinguish, categorize
Synthesis	↓	design, assemble, arrange
Evaluation	→ → ↑	judge, assess, defend

education to other "natural" environments. Furthermore, the skills and strategies necessary for the student's independent success in key environments should be the guide for goals and objectives targeted on the IEP. Thus, starting with the generalization skills, strategies, and environments can lead to a logical "plan back" sequence in which the desired end result, or outcome, is the basis for planning the individualized program and ongoing assessment process.

The IEP objectives should also link directly to the curricula for the general education students in a given school district. Special education instruction may involve basic skill, strategy, social skill, vocational, or remediation of deficit skill areas. Regardless of the decision made about the delivery of a student's instructional program, the context of success in general education curricula and return to general education classrooms (this will vary depending on the time spent out of the general education environment, appropriateness of instruction outside the general education setting) should always be the overriding goal of instruction. Thus, the objectives should necessarily be drawn from corresponding curriculum area(s).

Teacher efficiency in getting started with behavioral objectives that include content beyond basic thinking skills, generalization environments, and general education curriculum can be enhanced when teachers work in teams to develop and use common objectives. Special education teachers who consult and collaborate with general education, vocational education, and other appropriate personnel (e.g., parents, students) can develop meaningful and useful CBAs (Idol, 1989). Basic materials and their use are shown in the checklist in Table 2-4.

Table 2–4. Materials checklist for curriculum-based assessment.

Material	Use
Individualized educational plan	Determine CBA objectives.
Folders	Organize probes, graphs, and individual student CBAs.
Probe sheets	Gather data for student progress and performance.
Graphs	Depict student progress and performance visually.
Bloom's taxonomy	Ensure that low to high order skills are used (see Appendix B for verbs).
Curriculum guides (e.g., general education, vocational, social skill)	Refer to appropriate curriculum so that generalization environments are used to determine CBA areas.
Timer	Regulate the amount of time a student responds to a CBA.
Audio-visual equipment	Use cassette tapes, language master, or other audio-visual means to record directions, probe material, or student responses to CBA.

Comparing Teaching Methods

Fuchs and Fuchs (1992) suggest that educators use CBA to test hypotheses they have formulated about the success of their instructional methods. As increased research abounds within general education and special education, professionals actually have more opportunities to experiment within their classroom to determine the most effective and efficient instructional methods. This "teacher as researcher" model has been described in many areas (Allan & Miller, 1990; Lieberman, 1986; Miller & McDaniel, 1989) and actually empowers teachers to determine the *how* of what they teach by collecting data based on more than one approach.

For example, all 5th grade teachers may be working with the same science content, but one teacher may be using lecture methods with few visual organizers, another teacher may be conducting experiments with study guides, and another teacher might be using cooperative learning activities. If all of the 5th grade students were tested on the same content, which instructional method (or combination of methods) would be more effective? Within the context of the classroom, the same 5th grade teacher may use different methods to teach separate units within science, thus yielding a more tightly "controlled" research design, because teacher variables have been minimized.

Many instructional techniques have been well-researched and have well-documented support for their effectiveness: ClassWide Peer Tutoring (Delquadri, Greenwood, Whorton, Carta, & Hall, 1986; Fuchs, Fuchs, & Bishop, 1992), Cooperative Learning (Slavin & Madden, 1989), Strategy Instruction (Deshler & Schumaker, 1986), Direct Instruction (Gersten, Woodward, & Darch, 1986), Mnemonic Instruction (Scruggs & Mastropieri, 1992), and Social Skills Training (Epstein & Cullinan, 1987). Throughout this text, references and brief descriptions of methodologies are given so that readers can expand their existing repertoire and find ancillary sources.

Enlisting Student Involvement

Students with mild and moderate disabilities should be actively involved in their educational program. This involvement ranges from attendance and input during their IEP meeting (Van Reusen & Bos, 1990) to becoming increasingly responsible and independent in their learning (Graham, Harris, & Reid, 1992).

When explaining to students that CBA is going to be used, students usually need a clear distinction between CBA and testing. Because most quizzing or testing situations in school usually mean "it counts for a grade," students need to be informed of the purpose of CBA and how it can be used to help them and their teacher with learning and teaching. Furthermore, the act of involving students in graphing their performance encourages not only responsibility, but also motivation for learning.

Finally, students should be encouraged to set goals for themselves and to take an active part in scheduling educational goals and determining needed improvement areas (Fuchs, Butterworth, & Fuchs, 1989). Teacher feedback during this process can ensure that (a) realistic goals are set, (b) error analysis of problem areas occurs, (c) positive feedback for progress occurs, and (d) student use of self-evaluation increases.

Using Available Resources and Computer Technology

There are several material and human resources that should be used to ease the use of CBA. Some of these have already been mentioned, as in the listing of basic materials in Table 2–4, the need for teacher collaboration when developing and interpreting CBAs, and encouraging the involvement of students in the process. As software graphic programs become increasingly easier to use, teachers may find a variety of generic spreadsheets to convert student scores to graphs. Also, a variety of software programs have been developed specifically for use with curriculum-based assessment and measurement (see Fuchs, Fuchs, & Hamlett, 1992, for a description of the "Monitoring Basic Skills Progress" software program).

Developing Probes

Probes, as used in CBA and precision teaching literature, are the materials or procedures used to gather data for graphing on a particular CBA (see *Teaching Exceptional Children* Spring 1990 for a review of classroom practices for precision teaching). Probes may contain a listing of words to be read, a checklist of steps to be completed, a set of problems to be solved, or reading passages with questions to be answered. In some curricula, probes may be descriptions of teacher directions that prompt student's responses (e.g., story starters for written language probes), situations in which data will be gathered (e.g., work setting for vocational probes), or student behaviors that are contextually and socially appropriate (e.g., student interactions on the playground).

Examples of probes for individual content areas are in Chapters 3 through 9, with formats determined by the behavioral objective on which they are based. Teachers are encouraged to use and adapt the examples found throughout this text so that their CBA data are specifically applicable, meaningful, and useful for them in their educational setting (refer to samples of probe formats in Appendix A). Probe development techniques include:

- Setting up a measurement station in the classroom with probes for a variety of student levels and content areas.
- Developing a random selection of probes (i.e., Form A, Form B, etc.).
- Precounting the possible number of corrects.
- Using computer software programs that create and/or score probes.
- Covering material with plastic overlay for reuse after first use scoring and error analysis.
- Recording student directions and probe information on a cassette tape, language master, or other audio equipment so that students can individually and independently conduct their CBAs.

- Teaching instructional assistants, volunteers, or other school personnel to develop probes. Sharing with other teachers who are teaching similar objectives.
- Involving peer helpers or the students, themselves, in developing probe items and materials.
- Using checklists of student behaviors to serve as the measurement probes, such as with social skills or work-related behaviors.

Graphing Performance

The visual display of data from CBA may appear to be another step that can be eliminated to save time, but it is critical for ensuring that accurate and appropriate decisions are made about instruction. Furthermore, the visual display is a communication technique that clearly and concisely informs other teachers, parents, and the students themselves about progress and performance. Graphing includes:

- Using the same type of graph for all or most CBAs. Deciding on, or eventually developing, class-specific graph worksheets to provide a standardization of materials, making it easier to record, interpret, and communicate data.
- Involving students in scoring, graphing, and interpreting their data.
- Training instructional assistants or other school volunteers to score and graph student performance.
- Training students to set goals based on their graphed performance.
- Training peer helpers to score and graph student performance.
- Using computer software programs for data graphing.
- Setting aside time (for example, once every 2 weeks) to review graphed performance and make instructional decisions based on the data.
- Keeping a listing of alternative teaching techniques, materials, and other resources. When the graphed data indicate that sufficient and expected progress is not being made, the teacher can refer to these alternatives.

Evaluating Performance

There are several ways to evaluate a student's performance dealing with the criterion/degree component of the behavioral objective. Some of the methods used in single-subject research studies (such as trend, slope, quarter intersect) may be unfamiliar to classroom teachers. Nonetheless, they are useful for predicting progress (such as when designating IEP objectives for the following year) and evaluating the effects of a particular program (such as comparison of teaching methods). Other useful and perhaps less technical methods for evaluating performance are available (for example, make a decision after 3 days of data indicate that progress is not being made). The most important point is that teachers review their students' data and make instructional decisions based on these data.

Evaluation techniques include:

- Use of the 3-day rule. When sufficient progress has not occurred over a 3-day (or session) period, then revise the program before the 4th day.
- Target of a graph "aimline" (where the student should be performing after a period of instruction). A line is drawn between a student's current level of performance and that youngster's aimline. The 3-day rule is used to monitor progress.
- Development of peer norms. This can be as simplistic as targeting what the typical third grader should be able to do and setting that goal for a student or developing school-wide or district-wide norms that can be used in the assessment process. (See Shinn 1988 for a thorough description of how to develop curriculum-based local norms for use in special education decision making.)
- Determination of trend of performance by looking at ascending, descending, or flat lines of progress. Trend typically refers to consistent performance as indicated by three data points.
- Quarter-intersect is a more technical procedure that can yield a more accurate line of progress. First, divide the number of data points in half and draw a vertical line at that place on the graph. Second, find the mid-date and mid-rate for the left half of the graph and draw a vertical line. Repeat the procedure with the right half of the graph. Connect those intersections to determine the trend of the data (Alberto & Troutman, 1990).

USEFUL CURRICULUM-BASED ASSESSMENTS

Once a CBA has been developed and used, the process of returning to the CBA and verifying its worth is a process that encourages teachers to refine or revise the APPLY steps, if necessary. Curriculum-based assessment must reflect the aspects in the mnemonic USEFUL for both teachers and students. Educators can use the USEFUL query list in Table 2–5 as a CBA to evaluate their CBA for USEFULness. These questions prompt reflection, reaction, and possible revisions of a CBA,

Table 2–5. Evaluation of a curriculum-based assessment: Is it USEFUL?

Objective: Given the USEFUL framework for evaluating a curriculum-based assessment, teachers will evaluate their CBAs so that each of the six components of the framework are successfully fulfilled/accomplished.

U NDERSTOOD by others?

Students, Parents, Educators

S YNTHESIZE and communicate meaningful feedback?

Leads to future learning, builds on previous learning, improves current learning

E VALUATE critical objectives of curriculum?

Long-term, short-term, higher-order thinking skills, strategies

F ILL a present void/need within assessment?

Helps with instructional planning and selection of methodologies

U SE frequently to maximize instructional time?

Student involvement, increased time on-task, increased motivation

L INK assessment data to instruction?

Data used to make decisions about methodologies, student progress, and performance; data decision rules used

also further substantiating its valued enhancement of instruction. A fuller elaboration of the USEFUL mnemonic is:

1. Understood by others?

Communication of graphed results should easily convey salient curriculum progress to parents, other educators, and the student. Standardizing the types of graphs used, the information printed on the graph, and clearly labeling such items as legend figures facilitate communication of the information meaning. A CBA graph should display such minimal information as the behavior measured, assessment dates, and the behavioral objective. However, the information displayed should be sufficient to clearly communicate correct and understandable information.

2. Synthesize and communicate meaningful feedback?

If the objectives assessed on a CBA do not relate information to students and others that is critical to that student's success in school, the teacher needs to revise the CBA. Furthermore, a student's involvement in setting goals based on the youngster's data and understanding how personal performance relates to the data shown can lead to increased motivation and responsibility for learning. Feedback should include error analysis of specific problem types and awareness of student progress and performance. There should be explicit movement from teacher-directed feedback activities in review of graphed performance to feedback that is more student-directed and student-controlled.

3. Evaluate critical objectives of curriculum?

Within a school day, a multitude of instructional objectives are taught. However, the CBA should include only those objectives deemed important and decisive benchmarks for student progress within a curriculum. Teachers can construct CBAs that measure short-term or long-term objectives and need to ensure that whatever is assessed directly relates to instruction and is crucial for students' continued success within that curriculum.

4. Fill a present void or need within assessment?

If an end-of-unit test within a graphing period indicates that some or most of the students are not succeeding with the instructional objectives, teachers should use CBA to find out what needs to be retaught during the instructional unit — not after a low grade has been earned. The best of instruction is moot when students do not do well on a final test. Research of CBA indicates that teachers make better instructional decisions, more teaching changes more frequently, and increase student achievement and involvement in learning when CBA measures are employed.

5. Use frequently to maximize instructional time?

Short assessments are recommended for CBA to enhance instruction by its use instead of becoming cumbersome because of increased assessment time. Throughout this text, the use of CBA to ease transitions between content classes, review previously learned skills, increase time on-task when students are completing a CBA, set high expectations for student progress and performance across time, and involve students in their learning process are just a few of the ways in which academic learning time can be maximized when using CBA. Teachers must view CBA as complementary to instructional time, requiring active, not passive, obligations from both students and educators.

6. Link assessment data to instruction?

Making teaching changes during instruction is critical for helping students who are not making sufficient progress. Teachers are encouraged to develop a repertoire of alternative instructional practices, to employ different techniques when students are not progressing. Moreover, teachers need to involve students in this process to build a partnership between good teaching and good learning. Throughout this text, references to alternative teaching methods are given to provide teachers with means to try a different technique when data indicate that a change is necessary.

Teachers of students with mild and moderate disabilities should be able to substantiate their use of CBA by an affirmative response and rationalization for each of the questions in USEFUL. Improved teaching, improved learning, and improved performance are definite outcomes of using CBA. The remaining chapters provide examples of CBA in varied content areas and include suggestions to assist teachers in developing or adapting materials and processes for CBA to work well for them and their students.

SUMMARY

Educators who use the APPLY framework to develop CBAs need to also incorporate timesavers and resources — both people and material — to ensure that effective *and* efficient matches between instruction and assessment occur. Furthermore, the USEFUL framework can be used as a checklist to assist teachers in evaluating their CBAs. The remaining chapters focus on specific content areas. Even so, it is suggested that educators consider overlapping and integrating instruction and assessment recommendations found throughout this text so that the interconnections among applications in content areas can lead to CBAs that may be initially developed for one subject, but that can also be used to provide assessment in other subjects.

Teachers should start with one content, one group, one CBA —then revise, refine, adapt, and gradually expand into curriculum assessments that both complement *and* enhance all instruction and learning for teachers and students.

CHAPTER 3

■

BASIC SKILLS IN READING

SHARON P. HULLIHEN

■ ADVANCE ORGANIZER ■

Two major components of reading instruction are discussed: decoding and word recognition. Theories that have influenced the development of curriculum-based assessments (CBAs) for monitoring students within these two components are presented and emphasize the use of the APPLY framework in developing and using those systems for basic reading skills. Case studies, examples of student probes, teacher data-keeping sheets, and graphing procedures are described.

The acquisition of reading skills is thought to be the basis for most learning that takes place for students throughout their school careers. Reading can be defined as the translation of graphic symbols into sounds and words, coupled with the ability to gain meaning from individual words and word sequences. Reading is a process: It is the interaction between thought and written language (Weaver, 1988). It is the primary medium through which teachers conduct lessons or students acquire information in all subject areas (Cawley, Miller, & Carr, 1990). The ability to read, however, is not only crucial for success in school, but is absolutely necessary to effectively function in society (Doyle, 1983; Salvia & Hughes, 1990).

Reading instruction is generally associated exclusively with the elementary grades. Consider, however, that for those students who either do not acquire the essential skills through traditional methods or within the traditional amount of time, reading instruction, and, therefore, assessment must continue into the secondary classrooms. Further, even students in general education programs continue to need basic decoding skills, sight word vocabularies, and comprehension skills as they are faced with new vocabulary and concepts, as well as longer and more complex reading passages across all curricular areas at all levels of their education.

As more and more students with special needs, who learn in less traditional ways or time frames, are challenged by expectations in general education classrooms (caused, in part, by the federal laws mandating that students be educated in the most appropriate least restrictive environment [LRE]), more teachers across content areas are faced with the challenging task of teaching students who cannot read text material and/or cannot comprehend what they have read. Too frequently, students with limited proficiency in reading are expected to learn in content area subjects through a process in which they are already deficient (Cawley et al., 1990). No longer can we look at reading instruction and the assessment of reading skills as taking place exclusively within the reading curriculum and/or within a reading classroom.

In this and the following chapter on CBA in reading, three assumptions are made: (a) the teaching and assessment of reading skills takes place across curricular areas and at both elementary and secondary levels, (b) the targeted population for this discussion is composed of students with identified disabilities in the mild to moderate range, and (c) the acquisition and maintenance of reading skills are categorized into *basic skills* (decoding and word recognition), and *comprehension* (discussed in the following chapter). Strategies used by students to acquire knowledge through reading are embedded in case studies and are considered as content for CBA measures, when appropriate.

In this chapter, the reader will see that learning within the major components of reading can be supported by the use of short, ongoing assessment measures that can be used to improve instruction and promote student learning. Teachers use assessment techniques daily within their instructional reading periods without necessarily calling the measures assessments. Every time a student is called to read a set of flashcards or a passage from a book, or is asked to respond to a comprehension question, informal assessment is taking place. The difference between these daily assessment measures and a CBA system is that, frequently, teachers do not document students' performance and/or use the information to adjust instruction (Howell & Morehead, 1987; Salvia & Hughes, 1990).

Understandably, the teaching and assessment of reading skills might be less easily managed at the secondary level and across content areas by teachers who have not typically owned this responsibility (Armbruster, 1993; Cawley et al., 1990; Wilson, 1988) than at the elementary level in which the process originated and in which so many of the content areas have already been integrated with reading for instruction. With creative teaching and cooperation among teachers with varying levels of expertise in content areas and assessment techniques, however, CBA in reading can occur naturally within all classroom environments and at all levels. Teacher and student training about reading instruction, particularly at the secondary level with teachers who typically are not grounded in an understanding of reading theory or practice (Wilson, 1988), coupled with training and practice in informal assessment techniques will be necessary before any "natural" use of CBA in reading can occur at levels and within subject areas typically not focusing on reading.

Analyzing the reading curriculum in terms of basic skills, comprehension, and the strategies needed by students to be successful readers requires a basic understanding of the components of reading, as well as a basic understanding of learning strategies. Here curriculum refers not to a particular series or program through which reading skills are taught, but rather, to the actual sequence of skills students need to become proficient readers (Howell & Morehead, 1987). Scope and sequence charts for individual skills (generally in a hierarchial order) accompany almost all basal reading series. In addition, one can refer to teaching of reading textbooks for explanations of skills and their relationships to each other. *Reading Process and Practice* (Weaver, 1988) is used as the primary source about the teaching of reading for this chapter and provides a comprehensive look at the various components of reading instruction. If one is considering assessing reading skills within the content areas, a basic understanding of what is being taught in those subjects is necessary.

Analysis of curriculum should be conducted for students with mild to moderate disabilities as a precursor to the development of individualized education plans (IEPs) (Fuchs & Fuchs, 1986; Fuchs & Shinn, 1989). That analysis should not be an additional, but rather a natural on-going task, for teachers incorporating CBA into their instruction and de-livery of IEP objectives. Furthermore, once a teacher develops a CBA system that has at its core the academic needs of an individual student and an analysis of curriculum, end-of-the-year testing to determine if IEP goals and objectives have been met becomes both less time-con-suming and more meaningful.

Preparing items to match curriculum objectives in reading requires knowledge of both the reading objectives one wishes to assess and the content area objectives being taught to promote overlap. In the best of all educational situations, one is able to design an assessment that concur-rently determines mastery of both reading (comprehension or strategy use) and content area objectives. In addition, for students with identi-fied IEP objectives, the match must include (but not be limited to) con-sideration of those objectives. In the most well-written IEP, with objec-tives stated behaviorally, the evaluation criteria will already be linked to curriculum objectives (Fuchs & Shinn, 1989).

Frequent **Probing** to determine acquisition of reading skills can evolve into a natural process within instructional times (reading groups) as teacher and student understanding of curriculum-based practice in-creases, practice with CBA tasks occurs, and classroom management skills for implementing CBA systems become fine-tuned. Both basic skills and reading comprehension can be assessed within curricular content areas to create the most meaningful and legitimate CBA tools (oral read-ing of a passage from a science text; answering comprehension questions during class time about a social studies passage read orally or silently; using a "cloze" passage taken directly from a science or social studies text to assess comprehension). Case studies are presented throughout this chapter that illustrate this approach to developing CBA probes.

Loading data using a graph format and **Yielding** to results for re-visions and decisions about instruction can be handled with relative ease once a CBA management system is in place within a classroom and students as well as teachers become involved in the process. Making nec-essary revisions to the instructional process requires a complete under-standing of the complex process of the teaching of reading as well as knowledge of different methods of teaching those reading skills.

This and the next chapter are organized to individually address de-coding, word recognition, and comprehension (the major components of reading instruction). It is emphasized, however, that reading is a process involving the interaction of all three aspects for optimal use by a stu-dent for learning or by a citizen for existence in a world of print (Howell & Morehead, 1987; Salvia & Hughes, 1990; Weaver, 1988). Further, with training, practice, and patience, reading can be taught and assessed across all curricular areas and at both the elementary and secondary levels (Wilson, 1988). Throughout the chapter, the APPLY (see Chapter 2) framework is assumed and case studies are provided demonstrating its use in the teaching and assessment of reading skills. Frequent reference is made to the relationship between IEP goals and objectives and the curriculum skills being assessed.

BASIC SKILL APPROACHES

It has already been stated that basic skills for reading include decoding skills (the breaking apart of words into individual and combinations of sounds that are then blended together to form whole words) and word recognition (the fluent identification of whole words). Those skills are the foundation for most reading instruction. Without a system that allows one to decipher written text, no understanding of that text can occur. It is the understanding of written text that generally determines success or failure in academic endeavors after elementary school and throughout life (Howell & Morehead, 1987; Salvia & Hughes, 1990; Weaver, 1988).

Opinions vary about whether a phonetic (decoding) or a sight-word approach provides the best basis for reading instruction. It appears, however, that teachers of reading often choose a combination approach in which graded word lists (words identified as those read by most average students at a given grade level or those from grade level content area subjects such as science and social studies) are taught as whole words to be memorized for fluid recognition — generally within 1 second — and are taught concurrently with basic phonics skills (Weaver, 1988).

Unless reading is being taught through a basal reading series that actually becomes the recommended curriculum and dictates the sequence of sight words (controlled vocabulary) and of the phonetic skills to be taught, the analysis of the curriculum (choice of individual words and/or sequence of phonetic skills) is frequently left to the discretion of the reading teacher. In some cases, the school system has outlined a general scope and sequence of skills that teachers are to follow flexibly or stringently, depending on background and experience.

Although scope and sequence charts suggesting a hierarchical approach to the phonics skills needed by students to decode basic words are provided with most published reading curricula and/or from individual school systems' curriculum guides, many teachers make professional decisions about adapting a recommended sequence based on individual student needs. Students with mild to moderate disabilities arrive in classrooms with different combinations of skills than those proscribed in published or unpublished sequences of reading skills. In decoding words, for instance, a given child may have mastered some sounds or combinations of sounds which would typically be found at the upper end of the phonetic skills sequence (i.e., recognizing word endings such as /s/, /ing/, /ed/), although missing skills lower in the sequence (i.e., consonant blends or digraphs).

Therefore, an analysis of skills must be undertaken (pretesting) for each child before making programming decisions and determining goals. Pretesting can be conducted during normal instruction within the curriculum and can, in fact, be considered the first stage in the CBA process. One cannot assume, particularly when teaching students with special educational needs, that a child will naturally or necessarily progress through a given sequence of skills in a typical order (Salvia & Hughes, 1990) or in a typical time frame. In addition, one must not assume, again, especially on behalf of students with special needs, that because on one occasion a skill appeared to be mastered, that mastery will be maintained over a period of time. The use of frequent informal assessment of skills (CBA in its simplest terms) aids in avoiding this educational dilemma. Additionally, when writing IEP goals and objectives or when determining mastery criteria for a given skill, a maintenance goal can be factored into the recommended criteria. In other words, once mastered, mastery should be reevaluated over time and occur naturally within a classroom system for CBA. This is no more than a continuation of the ongoing assessments at the very core of CBA theory and practice (Fuchs & Shinn, 1989). For example:

Condition:	Given nonsense syllables with known initial and final consonant sounds and the short vowel sounds of /a/, /o/, or /i/
Audience:	John
Behavior:	will read the syllables (CVC)
Criteria/Degree:	with 80% accuracy on 9 of 10 trials
MAINTENANCE:	and will demonstrate maintenance once per month (80% accuracy per trial over a 3-month period).

Increasingly, in a whole language approach to reading instruction, reading skills are taught within recommended grade appropriate literature selections rather than or in combination with basal reading texts, and the teacher determines which phonetic skills are needed and which sight vocabulary is appropriate, based on the needs of individuals or groups of children. In these situations, teachers generally depend on their own knowledge of a recommended sequence of phonics skills or refer to a sequence from a commercially produced series. Some publishers have developed literature-based reading basal series. Refer to Weaver (1988) for an explanation and listing.

There are many commercially produced graded word lists as part of basal reading serials and informal reading inventories (Silvaroli, 1973; Spache, 1972), as well as several lists of frequently used words in the English language (Botel, 1978; Dolch, 1950). Some teachers of students with mild to moderate disabilities use these lists as a significant aspect of their curriculum, with the assumption that if students have not been successful in learning words from basal texts, teachers should put major emphasis on words most frequently found in any passage. Some teach the words from these lists through flash cards, reading games, or by putting words into some context, and then assess for the exact words that have been taught either in isolation or in context. Others teach from a graded reading series or from teacher-made lists and then assess from the commercially produced lists to determine generalized acquisition of sight words at specific grade levels. Obviously, if one chooses to teach and assess from the same lists of words, that process is far more in keeping with an attempt to test what is taught and, therefore, more accurately follows a CBA model (Fuchs, Deno, & Mirkin, 1984; Howell & Morehead, 1987; Marston & Magnusson, 1985; Salvia & Hughes, 1990; Tindal & Marston, 1990).

Increasingly more students are being expected to function with grade level textbooks in all academic areas (except reading), when it is impossible for them to benefit from those written texts independently based on the youngsters' lower-than-expected reading levels. Therefore, many reading teachers (especially of children with special needs) choose words from other subject areas as sight words in an attempt to make text that is written at a higher level than the student's reading level more understandable. Students who are reading 1 or more years below that expected for their grade level frequently require that type of support to benefit from grade level textbooks (Armbruster, 1993; Cawley et al., 1990; Wilson, 1988).

Additionally, those students who have been identified as having moderate disabilities (frequently falling within the retarded range of intellectual functioning) are commonly taught from lists of functional words (exit, entrance, stop, walk, etc.) that are intended (as the name implies) to aid individuals to independently function within society (Salvia & Hughes, 1990). These word lists generally form the base of reading instruction throughout the elementary and secondary school curriculums for these students with moderate disabilities.

Students with mild to moderate disabilities generally require more in-depth analysis of curriculum in determination of the most appropriate approach to the teaching of reading than do students without identified learning disabilities. That analysis is based on the underlying processing strengths and needs that aid in the determination of a specific disability and affect a student's learning. It is only after an analysis of how an individual child learns that a teacher can determine what elements of a recommended curriculum will best serve that child.

A traditional sequence of skills in a phonetic approach includes both the association of sounds with written letters and combinations of letters and the ability to blend those sounds together to form whole words (Howell & Morehead, 1987; Salvia & Hughes, 1990; Weaver, 1988). If a specific student demonstrates a deficit in auditory discrimination and/or auditory memory, a phonetic approach is almost definitely ruled out as a primary teaching approach for basic reading skills. That student either does not associate the correct sound with a letter or set of letters or cannot remember those sounds or remember in the correct sequence to produce a whole word. By the same token, students whose deficit areas are visual discrimination and/or visual memory will find the automatic recognition of words they see far more difficult than they would a phonetic approach to words (Carbo, 1983; Carbo, 1987; Weaver, 1988).

Obviously, a student who has difficulty in both areas of perceptual processing will experience a more severe disability in attempting to learn to read. Additionally, although some students with strong short- and long-term memories may find remembering phonetic rules (silent e rule, r-controlled vowel patterns, etc.) an easy task, those students with poor memories will find it almost impossible to make use of those rules to decode (or encode for spelling) words.

For students who fall in the mild to moderately retarded range, cognition is a major factor impacting their learning. Techniques that emphasize rote memory and the least amount of processing will probably benefit them most in learning to read.

DECODING SKILLS

The two primary components of decoding are sounds and blending (Howell & Morehead, 1987). Some sounds are individual or combinations of individual sounds (i.e., consonant blends /str/, /bl/; digraphs /sh/, /ck/) and some fall within structural analysis in which word segments (i.e., prefixes — re, un, or suffixes — ing, s) are taught as parts of words to be pieced or fitted together. The structural analysis component of decoding is actually a combination of sight (being able to read those word segments) and phonics (blending them with other sounds to form whole words) (Salvia & Hughes, 1990).

Assessment of decoding skills is frequently conducted with isolated sounds or the blending of sounds because of the very nature of those skills. To demonstrate knowledge of identified sound/symbol relationships, the student must simply say the sound associated with the letters or combination of letters. Blending skills are often assessed with nonwords to assure that the blended sounds are not known sight words to the student. Those nonwords, or nonsense syllables, cannot be found in text (Howell & Morehead, 1987; Salvia & Hughes, 1990).

CBA enthusiasts would generally support the testing of sounds or nonwords in isolation if, in fact, the skills had been taught in isolation. However, some current reading experts who support teaching decoding skills within the context of real words and real text (Weaver, 1988) may question the legitimacy of teaching or testing sounds in isolation or of employing nonsense syllables (i.e., nat, fim, uft).

However, it appears that students do require knowledge of letter(s)/ sound relationships to blend components into words within reading materials. Samuels (1976) notes that a sight-word approach to teaching reading does not allow students to generalize to new words in the manner that teaching decoding skills does. A lack of decoding skills accounts for many nonreaders (Anderson, Heibert, Scott, & Wilkinson, 1985). It is even less likely, of course, that students with mild to moderate disabilities will learn to read without a strong phonics base, because the youngsters do not have the ability to "discover" the sounds within the context of their reading and then generalize sounds for use with unknown words (Howell & Morehead, 1987).

It is important to remember, when considering how to assess basic decoding skills, that the ultimate goal of reading is not the reading of individual or sequences of words; but rather, to gain meaning from those word sequences.

Research supports that fluency is generally considered to be a mark of a skilled reader and that the converse, with less fluent readers having poorer comprehension, is also true (Carnine, Silbert, & Kameenui, 1990). Refer to Hasbrouck and Tindal (1992) for a discussion of *oral reading fluency* (ORF), which is the combination of accuracy and rate of reading. They make the point that neither rate nor accuracy alone are accurate predictors of a student's success in reading.

There are two factors that impede students in the acquisition of knowledge when their reading is not fluent and accurate: (a) unknown words interrupt the flow and, therefore, the understanding of text and (b) less information can be gained, even if slow readers understand what they read because they are not able to take in as much information per minute as fluent readers (Howell & Morehead, 1987). LaBerge and Samuels' (1974) model of automaticity in information processing emphasizes the importance of increasing the automatic (i.e., fast and accurate) decoding of words in text so that one's attention can be solely directed toward comprehending what is being read. Because accurate and fluent decoding of words is required for students to gain meaning from what they have read, then consideration must be given to assessing for fluency in decoding unknown words (Allington, 1983). Deno, Mirkin, and Chiang (1982) and Fuchs, Fuchs, and Maxwell (1988) established a positive correlation between fluency in decoding and comprehension skills. An assumption has been made that as decoding becomes more automatic, one is able to devote more attention to comprehension, and, therefore, understanding of written text improves (Potter & Wamre, 1990). Deno (1986) suggests that assessments of reading fluency can be used by teachers in setting instructional goals and objectives. Once these objectives are developed with reading rate used to determine baseline data, it would follow that reading rate would continue as the basis for CBA measures.

Some teachers believe that rate of reading (fluency) should only be assessed after accuracy of the skill has been established (Salvia & Hughes, 1990). This may be particularly appropriate for students with disabilities, who may be more subject to confusion and frustration more than average learners. This theory is incorporated into one of the case studies in this chapter.

In Table 3–1, Mercer and Mercer (1985) suggest rates for fluency and accuracy based on an analysis of several sources. Starbin and Starbin (1974) differentiate suggested fluency rates (accuracy plus rate) by grade levels. They recommend 50 to 70 words per minute with two or less errors for students in grades 1 through 3. For readers in grades 4 through adult, they suggest between 100 and 200 words per minute with two or fewer errors. Carnine et al. (1990) recommend even more specific norms in this area. A review of all recommended norms is in order if one is considering ORF as a basis for assessment. It is recommended, however, that teachers use these recommended rates only as guidelines and adjust standards as appropriate to individual student needs. When dealing with students who have disabilities, it is especially important to determine criteria for success in comparison to the youngsters' current levels

Table 3–1. Approximate median rates for 3 separate reading skills.

Isolated sounds	70 per minute with 2 or fewer errors
Words in a list	80 per minute with 2 or fewer errors
Words in text	100 per minute with 2 or fewer errors

Source: Adapted from Mercer & Mercer (1985)

of functioning rather than the normal rates for average learners. One can look at these recommendations then, as "ideals" and for the purpose of students' IEP objectives aim for a kind of "practical ideal" based on an individual's past performance.

The following examples of CBA for decoding skills are labeled by the actual skill being assessed. Each one is associated with IEP objectives band the components of the **APPLY** framework. Refer to Chapter 2 for a complete explanation of the APPLY framework.

Decoding: Case Study

1. Analyze the curriculum.

John, a student near the end of 2nd grade, has been identified as having a learning disability. He has not yet mastered all single-consonant sounds (although it has been determined that auditory discrimination and memory are only slightly less accurate than expected for a child John's age; therefore, rendering this a legitimate skill to teach). Informal assessment information reported on his IEP indicates that John has increased known sounds from 3 to 12 (from 13% to 53% of 23 possible sounds) during the current school year. Children typically master this skill in kindergarten or 1st grade.

In analyzing the curriculum, the special education teacher found that John had mastered such readiness skills as matching letters, naming letters, and following on a page from top to bottom and from left to right. He had also demonstrated an ability to visually discriminate letter forms and the ability to reproduce isolated sounds accurately from a teacher prompt. Sound/symbol relationships for single consonant sounds was the first decoding skill recommended in the scope and sequence chart that accompanied the reading series John's teacher was using.

The recommended mastery of 70 sounds per minute with two or less errors recommended in Table 3–1 would require John to accurately identify all but two of the sounds (an increase of nine sounds from his current functioning level).

John's teacher, Mrs. Harrington, decided that this level of mastery was appropriate for John at that time. Although it would only require him to add nine sounds to his repertoire, it would require a fluency component that had not been required in the acquisition of the previously mastered sounds.

Mrs. Harrington developed the following IEP objective and evaluation criteria based on John's needs in relation to the curriculum she was using. "Given 21 single consonant letters, John will name the sounds associated with the letters (including two each for c and g) with 95% accuracy on eight of ten consecutive timed trials and maintain that level of mastery for two trials per month over a 2-month period."

NOTE: Substituting 80% of trials for 8 of 10 trials would make these criteria less confining for a teacher by allowing for as many trials as the teacher chose.

- By not specifying in the evaluation criteria the format for the probe (given a page of 100 single-consonant letters, for example), Mrs. Harrington is also allowing for personal teacher judgment and preference in terms of the exact assessment tool that another teacher might choose.
- The maintenance component of this evaluation criteria is a bias of this author as mentioned previously in the chapter.

2. Prepare items to meet the curriculum objective.

Mrs. Harrington prepared a probe sheet (see Table 3–2 and Figure 3–1) from which to assess John's skills.

Table 3–2. Student probe sheet for single consonant sounds in isolation.

STUDENT PROBE SHEET
Single Consonant Sounds in Isolation: Form A

b	v	k	t	f	c	r	f	j	t
v	y	v	l	d	h	z	t	w	s
y	d	c	s	g	n	w	k	z	m
m	w	f	g	k	q	d	d	r	q
r	q	x	y	l	f	x	j	p	h
v	l	q	f	h	c	n	t	d	m
s	g	p	b	l	r	g	n	z	p
b	j	h	c	w	c	p	y	g	r
p	l	m	x	k	b	h	q	k	z

Name _____

Date _____

Mastery: Yes No

Correct: _____

PROBE SHEET

Single Consonant Sounds in Isolation: Form A

Objective: Given 100 consonant letters in isolation, the student will verbally identify the 23 sounds associated with 21 single consonant letters.
Directions: On the sheet I have given you, read the *sounds* that the letters stand for. Read the sounds from left to right and from the top of the page to the bottom of the page (demonstrate on student probe sheet). You will have 1 minute to read as many sounds as you can.

b	v	k	t	f	c	r	f	j	t	10
v	y	v	l	d	h	z	t	w	s	20
y	d	c	s	g	n	w	k	z	m	30
m	w	f	g	k	q	d	d	r	q	40
r	g	x	y	l	f	x	j	p	h	50
v	l	q	f	h	c	n	t	d	m	60
s	g	p	b	l	r	g	n	z	p	70
b	j	h	c	w	c	p	y	g	r	80
p	l	m	x	k	b	h	q	k	z	90
n	b	y	w	m	s	j	x	c	n	100

(Accept hard or soft c & g sounds in all cases. If the student does not use all 4 sounds at some time, note in comment section and reteach as appropriate.)

Number of sounds read per minute: _____ Comments:
Number of sounds read correctly: _____
Number of sounds read incorrectly: _____
Mastery = 70 sounds per minute with 2 or less errors.

Note: This sheet and the student probe sheet would have alternative forms.

Figure 3–1. Teacher probe sheet for single consonant sounds in isolation.

This probe was developed to test both accuracy and fluency of the sound/symbol relationships of single consonants. The recommended rate for isolated sounds (refer to Table 3–1) is 70 per minute with two or fewer errors. Salvia and Hughes (1990) recommend that probes be developed to allow for more than the recommended number of items read per minute, permitting a student who can to do so. The researchers further recommend that students be given more than one opportunity to respond to each item to determine, in analyzing students' performance, whether they can read a given item consistently. In this case, because there are only 21 letters and by necessity there have to be at least 70 letters on the probe, that opportunity occurs naturally.

Mrs. Harrington decided to use this probe first to assess accuracy and then accuracy coupled with fluency. Although the recommended mastery criteria for untimed tests is 90% or more (Salvia & Hughes, 1990), Mrs. Harrington decided that when John reached 80% accuracy on untimed probes, she would switch to a timed assessment as required to meet his IEP objective.

Because this probe is based on a long-term, year-long objective for John, the teacher has a choice of whether to use it throughout the year regardless of how many consonant letters have been introduced or to use more specific probes for individual or small groups of letters that have been introduced until all 23 can be assessed for mastery (Salvia & Hughes, 1990).

3. Probe frequently.

This probe can be administered by the teacher, an instructional assistant, or a peer or volunteer trained in proper administration as well as proper pronunciation of the specific sounds associated with each letter. It can be administered during a teacher-directed lesson in which each child is called on to identify the sounds as part of the lesson, during a tutorial session with one of the other assessors named above, or in a 1- to 3-minute assessment period, again, by any of the above named assessors. The probe can be administered as often as once a day, but should probably not be administered less than once a week.

4. Load data using graph format.

Regardless of when this probe was introduced, the data could be graphed to illustrate percentage correct or on a double graph showing two data points: one for correct words per minute and one for number of errors (see Figure 3–2). It is recommended that John load the data onto his graph himself, with or without assistance, and that the graph be displayed in a way that John and his teacher can easily refer to (on the wall, in John's CBA notebook, etc.).

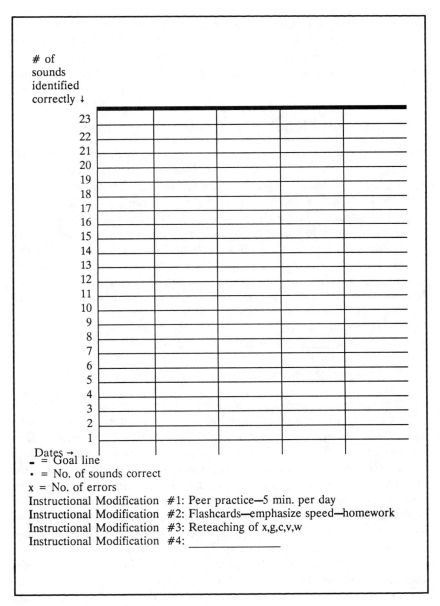

of
sounds
identified
correctly ↓

```
    23
    22
    21
    20
    19
    18
    17
    16
    15
    14
    13
    12
    11
    10
     9
     8
     7
     6
     5
     4
     3
     2
     1
```
Dates →

▬ = Goal line
• = No. of sounds correct
x = No. of errors
Instructional Modification #1: Peer practice—5 min. per day
Instructional Modification #2: Flashcards—emphasize speed—homework
Instructional Modification #3: Reteaching of x,g,c,v,w
Instructional Modification #4: _____

Figure 3–2. Graph for letter sounds.

5. Yield to results — revisions and decisions.

Because the teacher record sheet is designed to allow for error analysis (each letter will be marked as correct or incorrect), there can be reteaching of the incorrect sounds. If slow or limited progress is noted in attempting the goal of 95% accuracy on eight of ten trials, alternative teaching strategies can be implemented. If alternative teaching strategies are implemented, these should be noted on the graph as modifications.

Sound-blending in Context: Case Study

Sound-blending skills can be assessed in isolation through nonsense syllables (fis, aft, ifmabwot), or through individually developed probes using real words to assess mastery of specific decoding patterns, or rules, within the context of any reading material. The range of possibilities is great, but requires the teacher's knowledge of what skills a student already possesses. The following example will assess decoding skills in the context of science or social studies textbooks. Because a phonics-based approach assumes consistency of letter/sound relationships, when developing probes (lists of words, sentences, passages), one should be careful to incorporate only words that have regular and consistent letter/sound relationships (Lerner, 1985). When using actual passages from student texts, care should be taken to analyze student performance thoroughly in light of what skills are actually being assessed.

1. **Analyze** the curriculum.

Vaughn is an 11-year-old boy in the 5th grade who has been identified as having a specific learning disability. He has demonstrated mastery of all 23 single consonant sounds, all 5 short vowel sounds, 85% mastery of consonant blends, 95% mastery of consonant digraphs, and 70% mastery of vowel digraphs and diphthongs — all tested in isolation. Presumably based on his deficit in auditory sequential memory, Vaughn continues to demonstrate limited sound-blending skills within real words or nonsense syllables. His sight vocabulary is a relative strength for him, so many words have already been committed to memory and cannot, therefore, be used to assess sound-blending skills.

Vaughn's teacher, Mrs. MacTigue, notes that his inability to decode unknown words in text slows his reading rate and reduces his comprehension of text. She is also concerned that, as the vocabulary becomes increasingly advanced in his classroom texts, Vaughn will be faced with more and more unknown words. A pretest of Vaughn's decoding skills in the context of his science and social studies texts indicated that he was unable to decode an average of 50% of the words unknown to him (excluding those for which he was able to use context clues to decipher). An IEP objective criteria was written: "Given passages from 5th grade science and social studies texts, Vaughn will verbally decode unknown words with 80% accuracy on three consecutive trials and will demonstrate maintenance (80% accuracy — two trials per month — two consecutive months)."

2. Prepare items to meet the curriculum objective.

In preparing items for student probes, Mrs. MacTigue defined "unknown" words as those that Vaughn could not read in 2 seconds or less. Additionally, she determined that any unknown word that Vaughn skipped and then returned to after reading more of the text would be eliminated, with the assumption that he had employed context clues rather than decoding skills to read the word. Blending known sounds will be a focus of Mrs. MacTigue's reading curriculum for Vaughn.

The probe can be any passage Vaughn is called on to read from his science or social studies texts. Mrs. MacTigue has the option of predetermining which passages she asks him to read (giving her the opportunity to both choose a passage she judges as giving maximum opportunity for using sound-blending skills, and creating a data-keeping sheet that includes the actual passage) before the assessment or simply calling on him randomly as had been her normal practice. The latter does, of course, require the least amount of preparation time.

3. Probe frequently.

If Mrs. MacTigue chose to call on Vaughn randomly in class, she (or any other practiced observer) could "probe" his sound-blending skills as often as oral reading occurred. She could, of course, ask him to read a passage at any other time of the day, but calling on him during class time would clearly be the most time efficient. Mrs. MacTigue's data-keeping sheet could be a chart on which she could simply tally the number of correctly decoded words and the number of incorrectly read words. An alternative would be to keep a similar tally, but of the actual words.

No words read automatically (2 seconds or less) or assumed to be read based on context clues (comes back to correct a word after reading on) would be included in the tally. A percentage correct would be determined by dividing the number of correctly read words by the total number of unknown words attempted. The teacher's data sheet would be similar to that in Figure 3–3. Mrs. MacTigue actually chose to keep data not in a simple tally of correct/incorrect decoding attempts, but, rather, by writing not only the correctly and incorrectly decoded words, but also any word/s substituted for those read incorrectly.

Mrs. MacTigue decided not to consider reading rate as a factor for assessment in this case, although she was aware of the literature that supports it as a meaningful measure for decoding skills.

Name _____   Date _____
% Accuracy _____   Mastery Yes No

Objective: Given passages from 5th grade _____ text, Vaughn will
verbally decode unknown words with 80% accuracy.

Directions: List any word attempted which is not read in 2 seconds or less
and which does not appear to be read as a result of context clues.

Correct	Incorrect

Total words decoded: _____

Total words decoded correctly: _____

% accuracy = Total correct divided by total attempted

Mastery = 80% accuracy

Figure 3-3. Teacher data-keeping sheet for decoding words in context.

4. Load data using graph format.

The graphing system that Vaughn would load his data onto would be
a simple line graph indicating percentage correct and the dates of trials.

5. Yield to results — revisions and decisions.

As in the previous case history, Vaughn and Mrs. MacTigue would
yield to the results if an increase in accuracy was not apparent on the
graph. Because Mrs. MacTigue designed her data-keeping sheet to doc-

ument Vaughn's actual incorrect responses, error patterns could be determined and the related skills could be addressed within Vaughn's reading curriculum using new materials or the actual words that he missed. Additional teacher support, peer tutoring, additional homework, or rereading of the text used for the probe are possible instructional modifications that could be implemented and noted on the graph. Mrs. MacTigue and Vaughn would examine his graph once every 2 weeks to determine if instructional modifications or other interventions would be necessary.

WORD RECOGNITION SKILLS

Word recognition is defined as the fluent (generally within 1 second) and accurate identification of words in print. As students develop as readers, it is hoped that the need for decoding words is minimized as a sight vocabulary is developed and they are able to proceed easily through the reading of words, sentences, passages, chapters, and books.

Many students with mild to moderate disabilities have difficulty with the acquisition of a sight-word vocabulary at a level commensurate with the texts used within regular and even some special education classrooms (Armbruster, 1993; Cawley et al., 1990; Wilson, 1988).

The same theories apply when discussing the importance of reading fluency in relation to comprehension of text as presented in the previous section (Howell & Morehead, 1987).

Word Recognition With Words in Context: Case Study

1. **Analyze** the curriculum.

Tim is a 15-year-old boy identified as having emotional or behavioral disorders. His teachers report that Tim's ability to acquire knowledge from reading is greatly impacted by his lack of an adequate sight vocabulary. His word recognition skills as demonstrated on formal and informal test measures place him approximately 4 years below that of other students his age. Although accommodations have been made for him to gain information through other modes, it is problematic for him to attempt to gain information from reading his texts. Additionally, Tim's self-esteem has suffered greatly and he demonstrates a true desire to increase his reading vocabulary. At his age, Tim has already mastered words from commercially produced lists of frequently used words (i.e., Botel, 1978; Dolch, 1950) and can read words from 5th and 6th grade level basal reading series and literature selections, so his special education re-source teacher in his high school, Mr. Rubin, has developed lists of words from his 10th grade science, social studies, math, and literature texts. He works with Tim in a group of three students 5 days a week on words in isolation which are found in these texts. The students read from flash cards, play word games, work with the words in computer programs, and use the words in writing tasks as well as focusing on the meanings of the words through dictionary activities, word games, and illustrations.

Because Mr. Rubin is ultimately concerned with the meaning his students can gain from what they read, fluency has been considered as a factor in mastering these skills. Baseline data, which will serve as a starting point in the CBA system, indicate that Tim reads words in context with 60% accuracy when fluency (speed) is not considered. Mercer and Mercer (1985) recommended that words in context should be read at a rate of 100 per minute with two or fewer errors (refer to Table 3–1). When Tim was asked to read a passage in his science text, he read 60 words per minute with five errors. Based on his performance, an IEP objective was written: "Given passages from subject area texts, Tim will verbally read 80 words per minute with 3 or fewer errors on 3 of 4 consecutive trials." Mr. Rubin wrote this objective as a practical expectation for what Tim, the individual learner, could reasonably accomplish during one school year rather than aiming for a recommended norm.

2. Prepare items to meet the curriculum objective.

Mr. Rubin's probes were identified passages from Tim's texts. The teacher merely photocopied passages of at least 100 words each week from current chapters and "cut and pasted" the passages to become part of his data-keeping sheet. Tim read directly from his textbooks. Mr. Rubin's probe sheet is shown in Figure 3–4.

3. Probe frequently.

Mr. Rubin assesses students once a week in each subject area (science, social studies, literature) within his resource period with them. He could also have prepared the probes and asked the content area teachers to assess the students while they read out loud in class. However, it was determined that at the high school level, limited oral reading took place within class periods, so limited opportunity for assessment existed.

4. Load data using graph format.

Tim loaded his data onto a graph similar to the one in Figure 3–2 on which both words per minute and number of errors were graphed. In ad-

Name _____

Date _____

Mastery   Yes   No

Probe: Passage from p. _____ of _____ text.

Directions: Time student for 1 minute. Put a slash through any word that is misread. Circle the last word read.

Life is everywhere in the sea: fish and one-celled

organisms that you cannot see. Life is everywhere

on land as well: from deserts to snow-capped

mountains incredibly varied forms of life exist.

Each organism is well adapted for carrying out its

life processes. In this unit you will consider the

traits all organisms have in common. You will see

that at the cellular and molecular level the

similarities are even more striking. The word

biology is easy to define. Biology is the science

that deals with the origin, history, physical

characteristics, habits, etc. of plants and animals.

Number of words read in 1 minute: _____

Number of errors: _____

Mastery = 80 words per minute, 3 or fewer errors

Figure 3-4. Probe — Words in context.

dition, the goal lines (80 words per minute and 3 errors) were highlighted so Tim and Mr. Rubin could easily see how he was progressing.

5. Yield to results — revisions and decisions.

Mr. Rubin and Tim agreed to assess his progress biweekly to determine if instructional modifications were necessary. In addition, Mr. Rubin and Tim would decide together what modifications or interventions they would try.

Word Recognition With Words in Isolation: Case Study

1. Analyze the curriculum.

Maureen is a 13-year-old girl who has been identified as having moderate disabilities. Her school curriculum is based on functional life skills and functional academics. Her reading curriculum has at its core the reading of single words and signs she is likely to encounter and need when attempting to manage outside of her home or school environment. In assessing Maureen's ability to read functional words, her teacher, Mrs. Pitlick, uses flash cards with picture clues. Maureen has demonstrated the ability to read 12 of 20 functional words (words needed for her to function in society such as restroom, exit, entrance, etc.) 80% of trials, each word. The next logical step in a sequence of skills for students with moderate disabilities is to read the words in their natural environments. An IEP objective has been written: "Given 20 known words, Maureen will correctly read each word within the community — 3 consecutive trials — 2 consecutive months."

2. Prepare items to meet the curriculum objective.

The probe items were simply any words that Maureen had read correctly from flash cards, 80% of her trials, during a 2-week period. Mrs. Pitlick created a probe sheet listing the words she would be assessing and added words to the list as Maureen mastered them from flash cards at school.

3. Probe frequently.

Mrs. Pitlick decided that the probes would occur during her weekly trips with her students into the community (to the mall, the bowling alley, the grocery store, the bus station, etc.). Every time she saw one of Maureen's words, she would ask her to read it.

4. Load data using graph format.

Maureen loaded her information onto a simple chart by coloring in a block of the chart above the word when she returned to school. The block was left blank if Maureen was unable to read the word. Mrs. Pitlick dated each block. This charting system, although not a typical graphing system, made it easy for Maureen to see her progress and for Mrs. Pitlick to see when Maureen had shown mastery of a given word by coloring in 3 consecutive blocks. By dating each box, Mrs. Pitlick could keep track of the 2-month maintenance component. In addition, Mrs. Pitlick and Maureen kept a mastery monitoring chart to monitor the number of words Maureen had mastered toward her long-range goal of 30 words during the school year.

5. Yield to results — revisions and decisions.

Mrs. Pitlick and Maureen examined the chart together after each outing to determine how close Maureen was to getting 3 consecutive correct responses on each word. Mrs. Pitlick determined what, if any, modifications or interventions were necessary.

SUMMARY

Reading begins with the acquisition of skills in decoding and word recognition. Without those basic skills allowing one to decipher individual words, the process of reading for meaning cannot occur. Although the two major components of reading, basic skills and comprehension, have been addressed in separate chapters in this book, it is the interrelationship of the two that produces effective readers and learners.

Procedures for developing and using CBA within the basic skills component of reading instruction have been examined, with specific case studies presented that emphasize the APPLY framework for assessing skills in decoding and word recognition. The case studies are based on actual students with mild and moderate disabilities. IEP objectives coupled with curricular requirements are at the root of the teaching and assessment process in each case. Educators may benefit from applying similar procedures when programming for students with special needs or those in general education programs.

The integration of teaching and assessing these basic reading skills across curricular areas has been emphasized in an effort to maximize the benefits of CBA within a student's total educational program. Probes, data-keeping sheets, and graphing procedures have been presented as just a few examples of a multitude of possibilities. Any one of them could be modified for use with one or more students for the assessment of one or more skill areas to individualize this process for both students and teachers. The most important factor in choosing or creating probes or record-keeping systems within a CBA format is that it be efficient and effective for those using it. Educators are encouraged to make their own determination about how USEFUL their CBA is for them.

CHAPTER 4

■

READING COMPREHENSION

SHARON P. HULLIHEN

■ ADVANCE ORGANIZER ■

Reading comprehension is discussed as the ultimate goal
of reading instruction and the precursor to successful
functioning in school, work, community, and other
societal settings. Theories that have influenced the
development of curriculum-based assessments (CBAs)
for monitoring reading comprehension are presented
and emphasize the use of the APPLY framework in
developing and using those assessments. Case studies,
examples of student probes, teacher data-keeping sheets,
and graphing procedures are described and shared.

Once students can read basic written text with relative ease (fluency in combination with accuracy), they can begin to focus on comprehension of that text, which is, of course, the ultimate goal of reading instruction. It has already been noted and references have already been cited to support that many students with mild disabilities are faced with textbooks in which they have difficulty reading the text and, therefore, in comprehending what they have read.

Lovitt and Horton (1991) report a study by Lovitt, Horton, and Bergerud that correlated limited oral reading rates with limited comprehension in adolescent students who had mild learning disabilities. At the time, they were supporting the adaptation of textbooks for these students to maximize what they learn. More recent studies suggest that adapting or "dumbing-down" texts is one of the least desirable methods to use when attempting to make textbooks more useful to students. In addition, Weaver (1988) infers that many students can gain more information from silent reading than from oral reading because the actual task of reading aloud interferes with comprehension. However, students whose strengths are in the auditory rather than the visual area frequently benefit from hearing themselves read material if the reading is not laborious because of lack of basic reading skills.

Although in most cases we have been unsuccessful in providing students who have mild to moderate disabilities with textbook materials they can read, it is our responsibility as teachers to identify strategies enabling students to gain necessary information from currently published texts.

Although comprehension is consistently and sometimes painstakingly assessed, it is seldom taught (Ekwall, 1981). Howell and Morehead (1987) insist that some students have difficulty comprehending what they read for no other reason than that no one has taught them how to comprehend. This violates a basic premise of CBA: that what is tested matches what is taught.

Reading comprehension is generally broken down into the understanding of individual words (vocabulary development) and passages. Word meaning may, in fact, account for as much as 70% of the difference between students who do and do not perform well on comprehension tasks (Farr, 1969; Waugh, 1978).

Once students progress beyond the basic understanding of individual words (in isolation or in context), we break passage and text comprehension into literal, inferential, and critical kinds of understanding.

A student must have recall of details within text before we can ask higher-order questions that lead to inferencing, interpreting, generalizing, and evaluating (Singer, 1978), which are the ultimate goals of education. When, however, we assess comprehension by asking recall questions (which many teachers do), we place the emphasis primarily on a student's ability to remember, not to understand. In actuality, however, comprehension of material implies understanding (Singer, 1978), not memory.

Literal comprehension involves recognizing, locating, or recalling information that is actually stated within a text. Young readers and those with moderate disabilities generally demonstrate understanding at a literal level because cognition and experience are required for inferential and critical comprehension. Students are asked, at that level, to recall details from a passage (characters' names, setting, a stated problem from a narrative passage, factual information from an expository passage, or a sequence of events in a story or steps in a process), but are infrequently asked to use that information to draw conclusions or to relate it to personal or other reading experiences.

Inferential comprehension requires students to do something with the recalled information from text. Students are asked to analyze and synthesize information or draw conclusions about what they have read. They may be asked to describe actions or words that support a given character trait. They may infer cause/effect relationships or predict outcomes or next steps/events. Main ideas, paraphrasing, and summarizing are all included in inferential comprehension of text.

When asked to comprehend at the critical level, students are required to use the information they have gained from reading in combination with past experiences and text readings to evaluate or make judgments about what has been read. Frequently, there are no right or wrong answers at this level of understanding. Therefore, students are frequently assessed on how well they can support their judgments rather than their actual opinions. Students may be asked to construct a Venn diagram in which they compare and contrast similarities and differences between two characters, two stories, or two experimental results; to analyze an author's purpose or viewpoint; or to compare fact and fiction or fact and opinion. They might also be asked to use ideas presented in printed text to solve a contrived or real-life problem (Salvia & Hughes, 1990).

A teacher who is attempting to assess actual comprehension (inferential and/or critical) as opposed to memory (literal) would be well advised to focus on inferential comprehension and those attempting to assess students' thinking skills, focus on critical thinking.

A basic strategy taught to students to support their understanding of what they are reading is to have them develop self-questions at whichever level of comprehension is required. At the literal level, in which the answers should be stated explicitly in the passage or text, students might be encouraged to ask themselves: (a) Who are the characters? (b) What year was it? At the inferential or interpretive levels students may need to think about all the parts of a question and search for information to support their thoughts. Examples of questions students might ask themselves at the inferential level are: (a) Why did Jonathan lose his job? or (b) I wonder what will happen next? These questions generally have answers (sometimes implied) within the text, but might require information from more than one sentence or paragraph to be integrated by the reader for an appropriate response.

Analytical questioning from the teachers, such as (a) Why did the author write this piece? or (b) Were all of the statements in this piece factual? represent questions for which the answers must be found in the readers' own knowledge following reading. The answers will not be directly presented by words in the text.

Wilson (1988) suggests that too frequently teachers consider their reading instruction successful if students simply demonstrate mastery of basic decoding and word identification skills along with memory for literal information from a text. She reports that in such cases, students are generally only able to read well enough to survive in a given text or given reading activity.

Reading comprehension should be an active process (Orasanu & Penney, 1986; Pearson, 1985) in which understanding begins with the reader's use of prior knowledge as the foundation for constructing meaning (Spiro, Bruce, & Brewer, 1980). When we ask students to read for understanding, we are asking them to link the knowledge they already have with new information presented in a text. Gaffney and McCloone (1984) felt that students would not be able to comprehend on their own if they did not possess some background information on a given subject.

One of the strategies currently used with students to key them into their own background knowledge is KWL, outlined in Table 4–1, in which they are asked, before reading, to list what they already know about a topic and what they would like to know. A student, then, would be determining at least one purpose for reading.

Once students have made that connection between background knowledge and current text, it is important for them to become actively involved in understanding what they have read at a variety of levels. Al-

Table 4–1. KWL strategy.

K — What do you already *know* about this topic?

W — What do you *want to know* about this topic?

L — What did you *learn* about this topic?

though different names have been applied to these levels of understanding, students can generally be taught to distinguish between three types of questions illustrated in Table 4–2.

Some traditional forms of questioning such as questioning after reading and multiple choice or true/false–yes/no questions seldom promote comprehension and have limited use in assessing critical thinking (Durkin, 1978; Howell & Morehead, 1987; Johnson, Levin, & Pittleman, 1984; Osborn, 1984; Wilson, 1988).

Those who support the development of strategic readers believe that the complex process of reading comprehension involves a coordination of text features, task demands, and personal reader characteristics and encourage students to habitually employ these factors when they are reading (Paris, Oka, & Debritto, 1983). Because one must understand information presented at some level before being able to either recall it or apply it to other situations, one must understand the language used in the text. A consideration that frequently goes undetected when analyzing students' comprehension is their overall facility with language (Howell & Morehead, 1987).

COMPREHENSION STRATEGIES

Considerable thought and research has recently explored how students comprehend information. Also, strategies available to students that enhance comprehension of text can be observed within the assessment process and students can be held accountable for strategic use. All of the strategies support students' active participation in their own learning.

Strategy instruction includes teacher explanation and demonstration of a given strategy, followed by student practice. Sometimes these strategies involve cuing by the teacher or the use of a mnemonic to which students can refer. Some involve students working with each other (co-

Table 4–2. Types of comprehension questions.

Types of Comprehension Questions	
Literal	What does the text say?
Interpretive	What does the text mean?
Applied/Analytical	How can I use these ideas?

operative learning techniques) and others have students develop meta-cognitive techniques, such as thinking aloud or visualization.

When students are taught how to question within text, clarify for themselves while reading, predict next steps, and summarize for themselves during the reading process, they become active readers who self-monitor what they are learning with comprehension naturally fostered and improved (Howell & Morehead, 1987).

Cooperative learning strategies in which students work together to learn information and solve problems are particularly conducive to activating students' background knowledge (Flood, 1986) which is generally considered to be the foundation for comprehension of oral or written information.

Because there is increasing evidence that postreading questioning formats seldom promote comprehension and frequently simply fill hours of otherwise valuable instructional time with irrelevant work (Durkin, 1978; Howell & Morehead, 1987; Johnson, et al., 1984; Osborn, 1984), prereading techniques enhancing comprehension have become a favored instructional teacher strategy.

When teachers preview content and vocabulary and then direct students to read for the purpose of discovering or learning specific information, students are far more able to glean the relevant information often so difficult for students with learning disabilities.

With these techniques, students can be expected to read a given passage to find specific information, and, in keeping with the basic premise of CBA, they can be assessed on whether they have acquired only the desired or relevant information.

A simple technique for students to use when left alone with a text is to begin by turning the subtitles into questions and attempting to answer those before full text reading. Another prereading strategy taught by teachers and alluded to earlier in this chapter, KWL, which can eventually be used independently by students, requires students to do prethinking about the topic at hand by indicating what they already *know* about it, what they *want* to know about it, and what they think they will *learn*. Again, a strategy such as this puts students at least partially in control of the comprehension process.

Graphic organizers have also become popular means for encouraging students to understand written or oral text and come in a multitude of formats, ranging from webbing techniques to story maps to time lines. The graphic organizers offer students mechanisms to organize information in visual, pictorial ways. Both the process of completing an organizer and the visual representation that is produced help support students' comprehension.

CURRICULUM-BASED ASSESSMENT
FOR COMPREHENSION

The CBA techniques available to teachers in evaluating students' comprehension of what they have read are many and varied.

Questioning

It has already been stated that the most traditional and widely used assessment technique for evaluating students' comprehension for what they have read is teacher or textbook questioning after reading. It has also been stated that this assessment technique is probably the least reliable for determining students' understanding.

However, if postreading questioning becomes the CBA method of choice, Howell and Morehead (1987) suggest that:

- 5–10 questions per passage be developed;
- The questions be written at the same reading level as the passage, itself; and
- Yes/no questions never be included.

One of the concerns about the query method of testing for comprehension is that the questions have traditionally required nothing of the student beyond memory for literal information within the text. However, if teachers develop questioning pursuing more inferential and analytical information, perhaps the method's usefulness as a test of understanding can be improved.

One of the difficulties associated with this postreading technique, according to Pyrczak (1976), is that it is difficult to account for the element of any prior student knowledge. What did the student learn from the text and what was already known? One can control for the memory factor if students have access to the passage while responding to questions. Many students with learning disabilities have memory deficits that prevent them from recalling what they have learned. It is recommended that the following performance be considered for students when evaluating their comprehension of passages (Mercer & Mercer, 1985):

90% + = independent level
75–89% = instructional level
<75% = frustration level

Oral Reading Rate

Perhaps the easiest and most time-efficient comprehension assessment is by oral reading rate. Although this technique does not directly test comprehension of text, studies have shown a close correlation between the number of words read correctly during timed oral reading from text and comprehension (Deno, 1985; Deno et al., 1982; Fuchs, et al., 1988; Salvia & Hughes, 1990). This method, then, is more an indicator of a student's ability to comprehend, based on theories that more fluent readers understand more of what they read than being an actual test of specific comprehension of text. Oral reading rate is a good way to monitor general reading progress. It can be used easily across content areas, just as the APPLY example in the word recognition section of Chapter 3 illustrates. General rules for passage selection are:

- The number of words suggested for a passage ranges from 50 at the primary level to 400 at the secondary level.
- The passage makes sense on its own.
- The passage being read by the student for the first time.
- If taken from a basal reading text, the passage is taken from the middle of the text, as both the beginning and ending of basal texts are frequently review. If taken from a text in content areas, the passage can be taken from any part of the book.

Directions given to a student would be: "Read this passage out loud as quickly as you can without making careless errors." For ease of scoring, the student is generally timed for one minute; But, a teacher can choose to have the student read for up to 5 minutes. If the student hesitates for 2 seconds, the teacher provides the word and counts it as incorrect.

Cloze and Maze

The cloze procedure for assessing students' comprehension of text as well as for placement with instructional level reading material is another measure of choice based on its clarity of approach and ease of scoring (Baker & Brown, 1984; Baldauf, 1982; Berk, 1979; DeSanti & Sullivan, 1984; Howell & Morehead, 1987; Salvia & Hughes, 1990).

A cloze procedure is one in which a passage of approximately 250 words from a text is selected and then retyped, omitting approximately every fifth word. Proper nouns or numbers are not omitted. For scoring ease, there should be 50 blanks for a 250-word passage. The first and last sentences are left intact and the blanks are of equal length, so as not to provide clues to the student. To save teacher work, passages can be laminated in plastic for reuse. Instructions to students are simple:

- Read this passage silently or orally.
- Write in the missing words. Spelling does not count. (For a student with extreme graphomotor difficulties, saying the word to the teacher or other tester is an acceptable alternative — although, naturally, that process takes slightly more teacher time.)

It is assumed that students will practice this procedure so that it becomes familiar to them. Each sample or probe should be on a separate page. The test is untimed, but student speed or delay in completing the task gives the teacher diagnostic information. For a student who works relatively slowly, a time factor might be built-in to the assessment and graphing procedures to encourage speed, if appropriate.

Scoring is easy and reliable because one generally scores as correct only the exact word for a given space. Although these standards appear high, students are only expected to perform with 45% accuracy for the selection to be considered at their independent reading level (Pikulski & Pikulski, 1977). Almost anyone could score this assessment, if given a key. One scoring exception that complicates the scoring somewhat is that synonyms that do not change the meaning of the text can be accepted as correct by some teachers. If this is the case, the teacher needs to provide all acceptable responses on the answer key.

Students' performance can be assessed for placement into groups or results can provide baseline data on independent, instructional, and frustration levels (Ekwall, 1981). See Table 4–3 for performance levels.

One might choose to vary this procedure to assess for specific vocabulary words that have been taught or for a specific type of word or part of speech that has been emphasized in coursework (pronoun referents, verbs, etc.). In such an application, cloze is no longer strictly a test of comprehension (although it is clearly a factor), and words would not be

Table 4–3. Cloze and maze reading measures.

Cloze	Maze
Independent = 90–100%	Independent = 57–100%
Instructional = 60–80%	Instructional = 44–56%
Frustration = <55%	Frustration = <43%

omitted in a patterned fashion, such as every fifth word. In such procedures, one would want to omit an even number of words to make scoring as easy as possible. In addition, for less able readers, the first letter of each word or word blank, with initial letters for all possible responses, could be provided if desired.

Another variation on this procedure is the maze, which provides a number of choices for each blank. In this case, it is a multiple-choice kind of format, with students asked to identify the correct word rather than producing it — making a maze a much easier assessment task. Therefore, the criterion for performance is higher. The choices made by the teacher about what distractors to use determine the difficulty of the task. This procedure is of course, more difficult for the teacher to produce in probe format. It is a recommended format for students with language deficits, especially in the expressive language areas of vocabulary and word retrieval. Similarly, students whose primary language is other than English can benefit from this language aid provided in the maze format (Bensousson & Ramraz, 1984).

Retelling and Paraphrasing

Retelling and paraphrasing can be used both as legitimate CBA measures and as valid and traditional instructional strategies (Hansen, 1978; Schumaker, Denton, & Deshler, 1987). To produce a story-retelling (Kintsch, 1974) CBA probe, the teacher creates a list of the idea units found in a given story on a checklist. The student is asked to read and retell the story. The teacher (or peer tutor, instructional assistant, or volunteer who needs only to be able to read the items on the checklist) collects data by checking off all idea units recalled by the student. The directions for this procedure are simple. After reading the passage, the reader is told to close the book and pretend the evaluator has never read it. Students are encouraged to tell everything they can remember. During the student's initial retelling, the evaluator does not interrupt or ask any questions. Once the student has completed the first retelling, however, the evaluator can ask questions for expansion. One must be careful during the questioning not to provide information that the reader has not already given and should avoid yes/no questions. If, in fact, this type of questioning is acceptable, it limits the number of people who could serve as a scorer. In most cases, only the teacher would have the expertise needed to conduct the expansion questioning.

When asking students to paraphrase as opposed to retell a passage, the difference is that we ask them to tell the story in their own words. Retelling word-for-word indicates skill in memory — not in understanding (Howell & Morehead, 1987). Paraphrasing requires a well-developed vocabulary, making it difficult for students with language impairments in vocabulary or processing. A caution at the lower end of the reading scales is that it may be very difficult for students to simplify what they have read any further or to find another way to say it.

Fuchs et al. (1988) recommend that the easiest way to score a paraphrasing task is to tally the number of retold words. Another is to compute the percentage of words retold that are related to the content.

Howell and Morehead (1987) recommend that in using either the cloze or maze procedures, one also prepare interpretive questions to ask when the student completes the passage to compare students' performance between expansion and interpretation.

Sentence Verification

Perhaps sentence verification, the procedure most difficult to produce, score, and interpret is also the one that best controls for prior knowledge (Howell & Morehead, 1987; Rasool & Royer, 1986; Royer & Cunningham, 1981). The sentence verification procedure evaluates comprehension at the sentence level, but Royer, Lynch, Hambleton, and Bulgareli (1984) report evidence that this procedure is also an indicator of text comprehension. Sentence verification lends itself to providing diagnostic information to teachers based on the types of errors students make.

The sentence verification test (SVT) was originally developed to determine whether readers were able to retain meaning of text and whether the information in a given sentence had the same or different meaning as the one in the original text (Rasool & Royer, 1986; Royer & Cunningham, 1981; Royer, Hastings, & Hook, 1979; Salvia & Hughes, 1990). As in the other procedures discussed, the student is presented with a passage of approximately 250 words or approximately 12 sentences. After reading the passage orally or silently, the student is presented with one original sentence from the passage, along with three distractor sentences, specifically designed by the teacher. The student's task is to indicate which sentences mean the same as the sentence in the passage (identified by the student as "old") and which ones are different in meaning ("new").

The three distractor sentences need to be one each of:

1. A paraphrase of the original sentence;
2. A sentence with meaning changed, but with similar wording to the original; and
3. A sentence similar in length and complexity to the original and semantically consistent with the topic introduced in the passage, but having meaning different from the original.

The student is directed to read the passage and then read separate, teacher-chosen sentences and tell if the new sentences have the same information as was first read (Howell & Morehead, 1987). Obviously, students with disabilities in the area of language would have difficulty with such a complex task as would students with disabilities in the moderate range whose cognitive ability might not permit an understanding of the complexity of what is expected. Even a student with disabilities in the mild range may have difficulty with the organizational thinking involved in tasks such as this.

Word or Vocabulary Comprehension: Case Study

1. Analyze the curriculum.

Bob is a 16-year-old boy in the 11th grade who has been identified as having a moderate language disability in both the receptive and expressive areas. Although his basic reading skills place him above that expected for students his age on standardized reading tests, Bob continues to demonstrate weakness in the area of reading comprehension. He receives extra support at his school from the speech-language pathologist, who focuses on vocabulary development in all subject areas. His classroom teachers are aware of Bob's difficulty and also provide as many direct instruction and homework activities as possible to support these skills. Bob's comprehension in science and social studies has improved as a direct result of the additional help he receives. However, he still has difficulty when he's required to read material that is not taught through direct instruction (a novel for a book report, research material for content area reports/papers, etc.).

The focus of Bob's instruction to help him compensate for his disability is strategic in nature. He has been taught to scan his reading material and to write down any words he does not know. He then gets help from his language teacher, his peer tutor, or his parents to define the words in a way he can understand (dictionary definitions are too vocabulary-laden). Bob writes the definitions and gives them to his speech-language pathologist, who develops assessment formats using Bob's own definitions.

Bob's speech-language pathologist, in cooperation with his English teacher, wrote the following IEP objective: "Given self-generated lists of words from his independent reading activities, Bob will identify the meaning of those words with 80% accuracy and demonstrate maintenance on review tests — 75% accuracy — at least bimonthly."

2. Prepare items to meet the curriculum objective.

Mr. Altamirano, Bob's speech-language pathologist, developed simple probes in matching, cloze, and fill-in-the-blank formats as well as probes asking for the actual definitions Bob had given to him.

3. Probe frequently.

Bob was responsible for turning in one set of words per week from reading material of his choice. Mr. Altamirano administered the probes 2–3 days after receiving the definitions from Bob. Once every month or two, Mr. Altamirano administered a review test that incorporated words that had been learned since the previous review test. Bob scored his own tests using Mr. Altamirano's key.

4. Load data using graph format.

Bob's probes were scored on a percentage basis and he graphed them himself on a simple line graph which he kept in the language section of his notebook. Two separate graphs were kept: one for weekly tests and one for review tests. Because verification that the strategy was being employed was implicit in Bob's turning in of his weekly word lists, no data needed to be kept on strategy use.

Bob also received a grade for his assessments, which classroom teachers agreed to count as part of his grade for the class. This added incentive for Bob and demonstrated effort on Bob's part to his teachers.

5. Yield to results — revisions and decisions.

Bob and Mr. Altamirano agreed that (a) if he did not turn in the lists for 2 weeks in a row, a check system would be put into effect and consequences would occur each time after that point and (b) if his performance on Mr. Altamirano's weekly probes dropped below 60%, instructional modifications such as homework assignments or review with Mr. Altamirano during study periods would be added and noted on Bob's graph.

Passage Comprehension: Case Study

1. Analyze the curriculum.

Daniel is an 11-year-old boy functioning within a general 5th grade classroom who has been identified as functioning in the low average to borderline mentally retarded range of intelligence. According to both standardized test scores and classroom performance, his basic reading skills fall approximately 2.5 years below that expected for his age, and his reading comprehension skills fall 3.5 years below expected. Daniel demonstrates better skills in comprehension (only 1.5 to 2 years below expected) when material is read to him (auditory comprehension). Daniel's teacher, Ms. Henry, has designed his reading program to include a 2nd-grade basal reading series as well as literature selections that have been recommended for 5th grade students in her school system.

Ms. Henry has been graphing Daniel's performance for oral reading rate based on passages in literature selections recommended for 2nd grade readers to track his general progress in reading. In addition, she has been charting word errors during those assessments and has been providing instructional modifications and supports to increase Daniel's word recognition and overall reading rate. Daniel's reading rate with 2nd grade materials has increased from 40 words per minute with 10 errors to 70 words per minute with 2 errors within the current school year.

Ms. Henry has been teaching the 5th grade objectives in narration developed in her school system for comparing and contrasting characters within narrative pieces and identifying words and actions that support character traits of persons within stories. To achieve this for Daniel with 5th grade material, Ms. Henry, a peer tutor, or a volunteer tape record the stories for Daniel to listen to or read them to him. To test Daniel's mastery of these goals for reading rather than for listening comprehension, 2nd grade materials are used.

In addition, Daniel has demonstrated success with using graphic organizers to support his learning. Ms. Henry has used webbing, story mapping, and Venn diagrams within her reading and social studies classes.

Daniel's literal comprehension has typically been far better than his understanding of inferential content and Ms. Henry is interested in stretching his capabilities into inference. Daniel has demonstrated ability to name character traits that apply to individual characters and has, with direction, been able to identify a trait based on a concrete action the character has taken.

Because Ms. Henry assumes that Daniel's reading will continue to improve at approximately the same rate, she developed the following IEP objective: "Given 3rd grade level narrative reading material read by him, Daniel will demonstrate knowledge of character traits by completing a variety of graphic organizers with 65% accuracy on 3 consecutive trials."

2. Prepare items to meet the curriculum objective.

Ms. Henry developed probes which were blank graphic organizers, or charts, similar to those she used instructionally, with space allotted for the student objective and specific directions as applicable to a given story. In this way, she could use the probes for a variety of students and stories by simply hand writing the specific information on the probe sheet (see Figures 4–1 and 4–2 for two of many possible examples of probes Ms. Henry designed).

The number needed for mastery is left out of these probes so that the information can be specific to individual students. In Daniel's case, mastery would equal 4 of 6 items correct. The type of probing Ms. Henry has chosen actually falls in the category of questioning, although she has attempted to go beyond the literal recall frequently asked of students (and that opens the procedure to some criticism as discussed earlier).

3. Probe frequently.

Ms. Henry will probe this skill a minimum of once per week until mastery has been reached. Daniel will be permitted to dictate his responses if he chooses. Directions might need to be read to him.

4. Load data using a graph format.

Daniel will complete his own line graph to indicate percentage of mastery, with assistance if necessary. He will keep his chart in his CBA folder, which is kept in the CBA corner of Ms. Henry's room. Ms. Henry will monitor for mastery based on consecutively mastered probes.

5. Yield to results — revisions and decisions.

Daniel and Ms. Henry will evaluate his performance after every third probe to determine if progress is being made. If performance drops more than 20 percentile points in one probe, or if upward progress is not noted over at least two of the three probes, instructional modifications will be implemented by Ms. Henry and noted on Daniel's graph. Instructional modifications may include more practice with the probe formats, cooperative learning activities on the analysis of characters and their traits, or individual support from Ms. Henry in Daniel's reading group to emphasize character examination.

Passage Comprehension: Case Study

1. Analyze the curriculum.

Tara is a 13-year-old girl in the 7th grade who has been identified as having learning disabilities. Her basic decoding and word recognition skills have been successfully remediated through special education resource support over the past 5 years and are currently only slightly be-

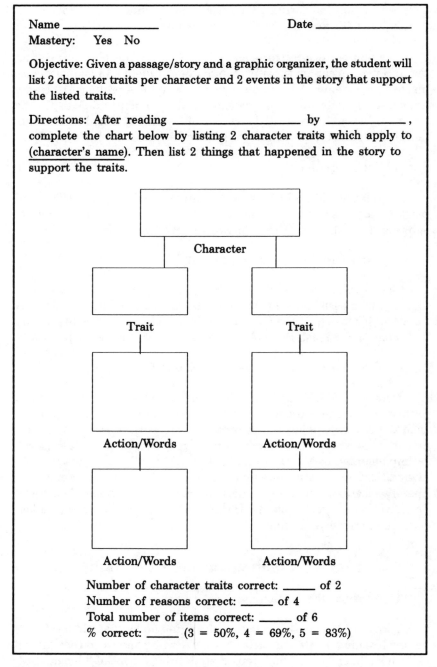

Name _____   Date _____
Mastery: Yes   No

Objective: Given a passage/story and a graphic organizer, the student will list 2 character traits per character and 2 events in the story that support the listed traits.

Directions: After reading _____ by _____, complete the chart below by listing 2 character traits which apply to (character's name). Then list 2 things that happened in the story to support the traits.

Character

Trait   Trait

Action/Words   Action/Words

Action/Words   Action/Words

Number of character traits correct: _____ of 2
Number of reasons correct: _____ of 4
Total number of items correct: _____ of 6
% correct: _____ (3 = 50%, 4 = 69%, 5 = 83%)

Figure 4-1. Probe for comprehension of character traits.

Name _____ Date _____
Mastery: Yes No

Objective: Given a reading passage about two characters, the student will identify 2 character traits for each character that are the same and different.

Directions: After reading _____ by _____ ,
complete the chart below which compares the character traits of (character's name) and (character's name). Name at least 2 traits for each character that are different and 2 that the characters share.

| Character 1 | Both | Character 2 |
Traits	Traits	Traits

Number of character traits correct: _____ of 6
% correct: _____ (3 = 50%, 4 = 69%, 5 = 83%)
Mastery = 4 of 6 correct

Figure 4-2. Probe for character comparisons.

low (less than 1 year) that expected for a student of her age. Tara's language processing skills are intact as determined by a speech-language assessment. Tara's cognitive ability lies in the above average range of intelligence. Her classroom performance as well as her performance on standardized tests indicate a strong vocabulary. Ms. Vogel, Tara's reading resource teacher (currently her only extra support in the general education classes in which she is enrolled), believes that Tara's lack of organizational skills (including preparing herself for reading tasks) as well as a memory deficit are hampering her ability to comprehend texts in all subject areas.

Tara's lack of comprehension skills for written text (she demonstrates good comprehension for material presented orally in class) is causing frustration and poor performance in her general education classes. Although she reads text material assigned for homework assignments, she is unable to successfully respond to questions asked of her in class or in written homework assignments that are based on that reading.

Tara's reading resource teacher has recently been teaching her some strategies that appear to be enhancing comprehension. Tara has been practicing "think aloud" techniques implemented when she realizes she is not understanding text while she studies at home as well as employing prereading questioning and the use of the KWL strategy (refer to Table 4–1).

Mrs. Vogel wrote the following objectives for Tara: "Given 7th grade level texts and literature selections, Tara will use learning strategies when reading cloze passages by stating the correct word with 60% accuracy and responding to inferential questioning with 75% accuracy."

Baseline data indicated that Tara was able to complete cloze passages at 7th grade level with 40% accuracy and she responded to postreading questioning with 50% accuracy.

2. Prepare items to meet the curriculum objective.

Mrs. Vogel has decided to assess Tara's comprehension with a combination of the cloze procedure and questioning at the inferential and analytical levels to tap the student's high cognitive skills. She developed cloze passages from science and social studies textbooks as well as 7th grade literature selections recommended by her school system. She follows the procedures as described in the comprehension section of this chapter in developing her probes (see Figures 4–3 and 4–4). Had vocabulary not been such a demonstrated strength for Tara, Mrs. Vogel might have chosen to use the maze procedure (also described in detail previously in this chapter). Questions applicable to the passages are placed on the reverse side of the cloze probes.

3. Probe frequently.

Mrs. Vogel decided to probe Tara's comprehension for actual text material three times weekly in a 10-minute individual session with Tara. She administers the probe with the direction to Tara to: "Read this passage aloud. Fill in all of the blanks with the appropriate word. Do all of your thinking out loud so that I can hear your approach to your reading." Mrs. Vogel has her own copy of the probe on which she writes Tara's responses. In addition, she notes any of the strategies she observes Tara using. Figures 4–3 and 4–4 are examples of Mrs. Vogel's data-keeping sheets (front and back). Tara's probe sheet would be identical, except that the strategy checklist would not be included.

4. Load data using graph format.

Because Tara's performance on both the cloze activities and the questioning are evaluated on percentage correct, both can be graphed

---

Name _____   Date _____

Mastery: Yes   No

Strategies used: Yes   No

Objective: Given a cloze passage, the student will fill in the blanks with 60% accuracy.

Directions: Read this passage aloud. Think of yourself as the author and fill in all of the blanks with the appropriate word. Do all of your thinking out loud so that I can see how you approach your reading.

My Uncle Bill was the best storyteller in the world. He was the first _____ tell me about Samuel Bellamy, _____ pirates who sailed with _____ , and their galley ship, _____ Whydah. My cousins and I _____ on the old nets _____ Bill's weather-beaten shack, _____ the fish and listening _____ his tales of the _____ . Bill had heard his _____ from older people, now _____ and gone, as they _____ turn had heard them _____ parents and uncles. I _____ my father laughing at Bill _____ he talked about the Whydah. "_____ hasn't been any treasure _____ there since a week _____ the wreck," my dad _____ say. "You never heard of _____ coming up with 30,000 _____ of sterling," Bill replied. _____ else would venture, it's _____ away. Add up all _____ people who have a _____ old coins, then multiply _____ by 250 years. "Gold _____ float," Bill would say. "_____ still down there. You'll _____ . One day somebody's going _____ to go after that _____ and come up a _____ ." Every old-timer on Cape Cod _____ his own idea about _____ happened. According to local _____ , Samuel Bellamy was a _____ British soldier seeking adventure _____ colonial Massachusetts. In 1715 _____ persuaded a wealthy patron _____ finance a ship, and _____ left the Cape with _____ crew of free men to _____ for Spanish treasure sunk _____ the Florida coast. Before _____ sailed away, Bellamy promised _____ beautiful young woman, Maria Hallett, _____ he would return. "I'll come sailing home, you'll see."

Total number correct responses: _____ of 50

% correct: _____

Check strategies used:
Thinking aloud
Pre-reading questioning
Other:

Figure 4–3. Data-keeping sheet for cloze comprehension probe.

Questioning to accompany cloze for comprehension.

Objective: Given a reading passage and 5 inferential questions, the student will answer 4/5 correctly.

Directions: After reading _____ by _____, think about these questions and answer them the best you can.

1. How would you compare the character of Bill to someone you know?

2. Why do you think Mr. Jennings wrote this piece?

3. If you had been Bill, what would you have done differently, and why?

4. In which dialogue between Bill and another character were you able to feel Bill's sensitivity toward his family?

5. Who would you say was the "best" character in this story, and why?

Number of correct responses: _____ of 5 (mastery is 4/5) = _____ % correct

Figure 4-4. Questioning to accompany cloze for comprehension.

on a graph similar to that in Figure 3-1 with goal levels for each noted on the graph.

Tara's use of strategies can be documented with a check across the horizontal axis of the graph for each date on which Mrs. Vogel determines that the student chose and used appropriate strategies to support her comprehension.

5. Yield to results — revisions and decisions.

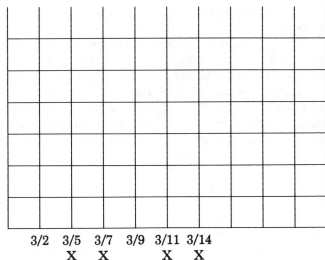

	3/2	3/5	3/7	3/9	3/11	3/14
Strategy Used		X	X		X	X

Mrs. Vogel and Tara will evaluate her progress once a week and will together decide when modifications are necessary and which ones would be helpful.

SUMMARY

Reading is a complex process in which teachers and students interact at various levels and across curricular areas throughout the total educational experience. In this and the previous chapter, that process has been delineated by examining and interrelating the individual skill areas of decoding, word recognition, and comprehension. In this chapter, major emphasis has been placed on comprehension (understanding, not memory) of written text as an ultimate goal of education and as the foundation for successful functioning in school, work, community, and other societal settings.

Procedures for developing and using CBA of student performance in reading comprehension has been examined. Specific case studies have been presented emphasizing the APPLY framework within the teaching of reading. The case studies are based on true stories of students with mild and moderate disabilities. IEP objectives drive the teaching and assessment process, as well as its link to curriculum. Educators may find it useful to use similar procedures with students who may be at-risk for learning problems or simply to monitor programming for students in general.

Emphasis has been placed on integrating the teaching and assessing of reading skills into all curricular areas in an effort to maximize the benefits of the CBA process. Moreover, teachers are encouraged to "mix and match" the probes, data-keeping sheets, and graphing procedures with others presented throughout this text. Teacher objectives *must* include USEFUL CBA systems so that student and teacher needs are met in an efficient and effective manner.

CHAPTER 5

■

WRITTEN LANGUAGE

■ ADVANCE ORGANIZER ■

The purpose of this chapter is to describe curriculum-based assessments (CBAs) in written language that span elementary and secondary grades. Research with students with mild and moderate disabilities suggests that direct instruction in writing mechanics and processes are essential building blocks for developing effective and functional proficiency in written language. CBA prototypes are provided, along with suggestions for incorporating other curricula and meaningful experiences into written language instruction and assessment.

L anguage development is a cornerstone for many areas of content in elementary and secondary programs. Among the factors considered when teaching new units of instruction are a student's experiential background, familiarity with vocabulary, and ability to convey new learning through verbal or written interactions. Thus, the influences of culture, previous experiences, and prior instruction in word knowledge, meanings, and usage in spoken and written language present a dynamic and diverse basis for educational instruction and assessment in these areas (Franklin, 1992).

This chapter includes several fundamental aspects of written language: spoken language, letter identification and formation, word identification and spelling, sentence writing, paragraph writing, and writing for a purpose. Wesson, Otis-Wilborn, Hasbrouck, and Tindal (1989) recommend linking assessment, curriculum, and instruction of both oral and written language samples for students with mild and moderate disabilities. They suggest that CBA research has sensitized educators to reflecting on both the progress of their students *and* the effectiveness of instructional methods.

Additionally, Tindal and Parker (1991) advise that four requirements be adhered to when developing a writing assessment method. Regardless of the purpose of assessment (see Chapters 1 and 2), the writing assessment method should:

1. Be administered consistently and scored reliably,
2. Discriminate among learners from varied skill levels,
3. Be at least moderately related to other accepted assessment methods, and
4. Depict score improvement by students during a school year.

Educators should match their CBAs to each of these criteria so that more reliable, valid, and sensitive written language measures are generated.

At the conclusion of this chapter, researched methods for written language instruction are presented in Table 5–5 as possible instructional alternatives to enhance writing products for students with mild and moderate disabilities.

SPOKEN LANGUAGE

Repeated emphasis on a student's use of speaking a language before writing a language are even more evident as schools serve increasingly diverse populations with cultural influences from varied native language backgrounds. Developmental milestones for native English-speaking students may vary from those appropriate for students who are learning English as their second language and especially vary for those students who are labeled as having learning problems concurrent with learning a new language. Consequently, the acquisition and use of speaking as a communication tool requires a comprehensive assessment that incorporates informal and situational results (for example, transcribing a child's verbal interactions while playing).

Franklin (1992) states that African-American students with disabilities may have language and dialectical differences reflecting important cultural influences affecting both spoken and written communication. She reminds educators that cultural sensitivity must be a part of an assessment and instructional process. Students should not be automatically characterized as answering incorrectly or being academically incompetent if they are displaying responses or behaviors that are diverse based on cultural or linguistic differences.

Ortiz and Wilkinson (1991) suggest that teachers of students who use English as a second language examine student performance in both English and the youngster's native language. In this way, CBA results can demonstrate if a student's presumed deficit area in spoken language is related to their language background or to a disability.

LETTER IDENTIFICATION AND FORMATION

In the primary grades, identifying and writing letters are considered basic skill areas that transfer into writing hand printed or cursive words and then forming sentences and paragraphs of written language. Goals and objectives on students' IEPs may deal with verbally identifying letters of the alphabet, writing teacher-dictated letters and words correctly, and forming words that are legible and correctly spelled.

Graham (1992) presents an analysis of handwriting instruction for students with mild and moderate disabilities in the elementary grades and concludes with several notes on the efficacy of handwriting instruction. Among his points are (a) the lack of empirical information favoring the teaching of slanted manuscript over traditional manuscript letters, (b) the need for direct instruction as a proactive means of handwriting instruction as well as reteaching during the context of meaningful writing experiences, and (c) the use of self-regulation (for example, self-evaluation, goal-setting, self-reinforcement) during the writing process to enhance performance. Furthermore, an emphasis on handwriting instruction that focuses on legibility and fluency as well as correction of and reteaching typical error patterns are issues that permeate Graham's work.

Within CBA, handwriting may be measured initially through letter reproduction with a model, letter reproduction from memory, and letter linkage to correctly form a word. The elements addressed in the criterion portion of the behavioral objective include print that is (a) within the line guidelines, (b) appropriate slant, (c) correct formation, and (d) printed quickly. Instruction in a writing program may emphasize the mechanics of letter formation, although the CBA throughout the instruction may focus on the number of correctly formed letters written from memory during a 1-minute dictation exercise. The following example shows how a teacher uses the APPLY framework to develop and use a CBA for writing with 1st grade students.

Letter Formation: Case Study

1. Analyze the curriculum.

The curriculum objective for 1st graders states that students must be able to correctly form upper and lower case letters. Based on the average rate of performance from other 1st grade students in her school (i.e., the "norm"), Ms. Atkinson determines that the typical rate is 42 letters per minute. The behavioral objective guiding the preparation of materials and procedures for this CBA is: "Given lined writing paper, a pencil, and teacher directions to write a letter of the alphabet, the student will correctly write the dictated letter at a rate of 42 letters per minute."

2. Prepare items to meet the curriculum objectives.

Ms. Atkinson has 52 letters to choose from for each dictated listing of letters — 26 lower case letters and 26 upper case letters. To choose the broadest listing of items to assess her objective, Ms. Atkinson has prepared a deck of cards that can be shuffled, for a random sampling of the 52 letters to be easily available for each assessment. This procedure also promotes increasing proficiency and fluency in letter writing, because the measure encompasses a unit of instruction (all letters) versus individual skills (only assessing letters being instructed on during a given week) within the unit.

3. Probe frequently.

On Tuesday and Thursday mornings, just before her formal language arts instruction begins, Ms. Atkinson has each student take out a sheet of paper and a pencil to practice their writing fluency with the letters. The teacher dictates at a rate of one letter every 5 seconds, but the students have been well instructed in how to take this probe — they know they are to write the last letter they have heard. That is, a student who is still forming a letter when hearing the next letter may skip a letter heard and then wait for the next letter they hear. Additionally, the students are encouraged to correctly write the letters they know — that if they hear a letter that they cannot yet write (and these letters may be ones that have not yet been given in direct instruction) they may skip that letter and wait until the next letter is called.

4. Load data using a graph format.

At the end of the week, Ms. Atkinson scores and graphs each student's paper (see Figure 5–1) and makes notes in her plans for the following week about which letters she may need to reteach in the following week (see Table 5–1 of her Error Analysis Chart).

5. Yield to results — revisions and decisions.

Thomas, a student with mild learning disabilities and fine motor problems, forms his letters correctly but is not achieving at the same rate as the other students. Because he appears to have mastered formation aspects of letter writing, Ms. Atkinson decides to conference with him the following Monday morning to (a) praise his correct letter formation, (b) provide feedback about the pace of his writing, and (c) prompt him to set a goal for increasing his fluency.

Adaptations of the APPLY example in letter identification and formation can be used to develop CBAs in spelling words, vocabulary definitions, or other curriculum areas. The next section focuses on spelling within written language.

SPELLING

According to data compiled by *U.S. News and World Report* (Database, May 18, 1992, p. 12), there are 40 sounds in the English language and more than 550 ways to spell those sounds. Rules and guidelines for *which* way to spell sounds frequently boils down to students' memorizing correct spellings. Obviously, problems in spelling competence are compounded when students have memory problems, which is typical of students with mild and moderate disabilities.

Frazier and Paulson (1992) suggest that students who do not like to write also have problems with handwriting and spelling, and, conse-

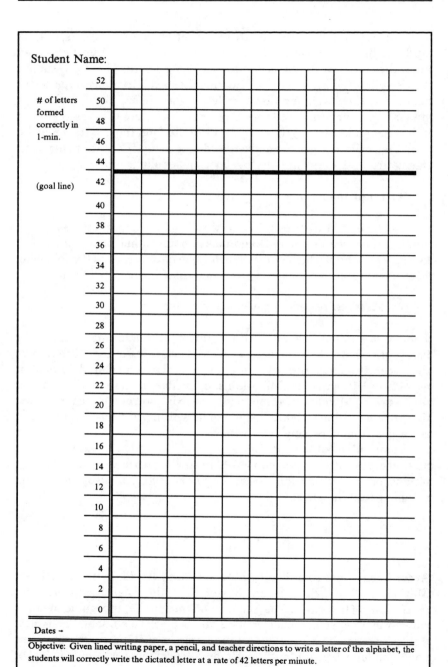

Figure 5–1. Graph of letter formation.

Table 5-1. Error analysis worksheet for letter formation.

Type of Error	Number of Occurrences*
Formed letter /e/ incorrectly	LJ, CK, TD, RS
Substituting /b/ for /d/	TD, MS, HI
Increase fluency	All students except MH, RE, SK

* Use of student's initials helps to form groups for reteaching or peer helping.

quently, have little motivation for doing well — or better — in writing. A systematic program in spelling employing CBA to both measure and analyze student errors provides teachers with specific instructional information. The student's score on a spelling test or probe provides useful quantitative information, but it is also necessary to categorize the types of errors made to allow for corrective instruction. When instruction and assessment are intertwined, then direct feedback to students combined with involvement in their spelling strengths and remediation need areas occur, there is increased potential for student motivation and performance.

The importance of conducting error analysis, versus simply viewing a graph, is illustrated by Fuchs, Fuchs, Hamlett, and Allinder (1991a). They found that teachers who used computerized data collection, which automatically administers and scores student's spelling, prevented teachers from making critical instructional decisions about student response patterns. Although using computer software is a timesaver for teachers, it must be used within the broad context of instructional analysis of student error patterns. The following example of APPLY uses one approach to obtain direct and frequent measurement of student success in spelling, as well as utilization of student error patterns to make decisions about the student's instructional programming.

Spelling: Case Study

1. **Analyze** the curriculum.

Long-term goals for CBA in spelling include the words a student is expected to spell within a year's amount of time (Fuchs, Fuchs, Hamlett, & Allinder, 1991b). Mr. Walsh randomly selects five sets of 25 words from the 3rd grade curriculum, which is the curriculum designated for his students with mild and moderate disabilities. By establishing five sets of the year's curriculum, Mr. Walsh is able to sample student performance throughout the year by using different forms of the same global set of words (i.e., the 3rd grade curriculum). His objective reads "Given 25 words randomly selected from the 3rd grade curriculum, the student will correctly spell each word."

2. Prepare items to meet the objective.

Because the curriculum for spelling in the 3rd grade is constructed in a week-by-week fashion focusing on spelling patterns, Mr. Walsh decides to select every 12th word for the first set — or probe, then the next word for the second set, and so on. By the time Mr. Walsh has completed this task he is set for the year with five probes of the 3rd grade spelling curriculum.

3. Probe frequently.

Each Wednesday the students complete a spelling probe requiring them to spell each of the 25 words "the best that they can" within a 2-minute time period. Mr. Walsh makes it clear that some of the words have not yet been taught, so students should not feel discouraged when they do not know how to spell such a word.

4. Load data using a graph format.

Mr. Walsh can collect data in one of two ways. The first way is a traditional method for collecting spelling data and that is to give credit only when a whole word is spelled correctly. The second way is typically associated with a procedure called "precision teaching," and requires a more sensitive measure. This measure is the number of correct letter sequences, giving students credit for the number of correct sequences within a word (see Table 5-2 for directions for scoring correct letter sequences). Mr. Walsh decides to use the traditional method for scoring words correct, with students receiving one point of credit for each word spelled entirely correctly. Refer to Appendix B for samples of graphs that can be used to record data.

5. Yield to results — revisions and decisions.

After scoring each student's work and plotting the data on the graph, Mr. Walsh then makes notations about the types of spelling errors students are making. If the types of errors are from a unit in spelling that has already been taught, then Mr. Walsh knows he needs to return

Table 5-2. Scoring correct letter or word sequences.

Correct Letter or Word Sequences (CLS or CWS)

Definition: Two adjacent, correctly spelled words that are grammatically
                     acceptable within the context of the phrase.

To score: 1. Carat (∧) correct sequences.
                     2. Invert carat (∨) incorrect sequences (invert before and
                        after misspelled words).
                     3. Include carats into and out of sentence.
                     4. Divide the number of CWS by the total number of
                        sequences to get the proportion of CWS.

Variations: Decide if punctuation, capitalization, or other aspects of writing will be scored as
errors.

Source: Shinn, M., & Tilly, W. D. (1989). *CBA Summer Institute 1989.* Eugene: University
of Oregon.

to that area and reteach. Because he notices that different students are
remembering different spelling patterns, he enlists student assistance
through the use of peer tutoring, to share the responsibility for reteaching.

WRITING SENTENCES AND PARAGRAPHS

The ability to write a sequence of sentences about a main topic is required throughout the school career including writing descriptive paragraphs to report factual information, responding to short answer or
essay questions on tests, and preparing persuasive paragraphs that are
intended to convince an audience of a view. The goals of written language include measures of student success in the school curriculum
(e.g., writing book reports), student success outside the school (e.g., describing previous work experience for a potential employer), and ex-
pressing creativity (e.g., developing a point of view about a current topic).

CBAs typically begin with a story starter that sets the context and
prompts students to complete the scenario independently (Deno, 1985).
Usually this verbal prompt is given by the teacher and is preceded by an
advance organizer that directs students to listen carefully, think for a
minute about possible endings, and write creatively to complete the
story. A variation of a story starter is a story ender with goal-directed
prompts for generating content (Montague, Graves, & Leavell, 1991).

The quantitative and qualitative measures that a teacher chooses for scoring the written products reflect the importance of the mechanics and style of writing that the teacher has set up as criterion for writing objectives. Fluency with a writing task, vocabulary used, structure of the sentences, and the content of a paragraph are examples of items that teachers may target for scoring a written product. Table 5–3 compiles various scoring schemas that teachers may choose from.

Portfolios that contain samples of student work in writing is one organizational method for compiling information about student performance. Frazier and Paulson (1992) report that student involvement in selecting work that goes in their portfolio can increase motivation and responsibility for improving their writing. First, students must become familiar with how their work is to be judged. Next, students are required to choose their best pieces of work for evaluation. Finally, students are involved in the evaluation process, which encourages ownership, reflection on their work, and setting goals for the areas they want to improve in.

Written Language: Case Study

1. Analyze the curriculum.

Mr. Johnson's junior high English class is practicing writing with a literature book they are reading as the context. After each chapter, the students must summarize the content in a series of paragraphs. Mr. Johnson has recently read about some research (Sawyer, Graham, & Harris, 1992) in which students were taught a strategy for writing. Because successful results were reported in this research, Mr. Johnson decided to use the strategy — not only in his instruction but, also, as the scoring measure. His objective is: "After reading a chapter from the literature book, the student will write at least two paragraphs that summarize the chapter using the W-W-W, What = 2, How = 2 strategy for improvement of a student's story grammar and quality of writing."

2. Prepare items to meet the objectives.

The strategy steps are: (1) Who is the main character? Who else is in the story? (2) When does the story take place? (3) Where does the story take place? (4) What does the main character want to do? (5) What happens when he or she tries to do it? (6) How does the story end? (7) How does the main character feel? If a student uses the strategy correctly, then the story grammar score should be high. Graham and Harris (1989) designed the Story Element Scale (see Table 5–4) for scoring story grammar.

Table 5–3. Qualitative and quantitative scoring units for written language.

Qualitative	Quantitative
Fluency	

Rate samples of writing for
  language level
  message quality
  directional features
	Rate samples of writing for
	  total number of words
	  average sentence length
	  variety of sentence types

Content	

Rate samples of writing for
  idea generation
  coherence
  organization
  awareness of audience
	Rate samples of writing for
	  accuracy
	  ideas
	  organization
	  0 to 10 rating scale

Conventions/Structure	

Analyze writing for
  errors that interfere with message
	Analyze writing for
	  spelling
	  punctuation
	  handwriting
	  grammar
	  correct word sequence
	  grammatical correctness
	  error analysis chart
	  frequency of error types

Syntax	

Analyze sentence forms for
  variation in the use of patterns
  first expansions (NP + VP +
   NP, conjunctions)
  transformations (relative and
   subordinate clauses)
	Analyze writing for
	  T-unit length
	  syntactic density score
	  variety of sentence types

Vocabulary	

Identify words
  not used before
  overused
  used inappropriately
	Identify
	  large words
	  unrepeated words
	  low-frequency words
	  type-token ratio
	  index of diversification

Sources: Isaacson, S. (1988). Assessing the writing product: Qualitative and quantitative measures. *Exceptional Children, 54,* 528–534; Mercer, C. D., & Mercer A. (1985). Teaching handwriting and written expression skills in *Teaching students with learning problems* (2nd ed.). Columbus, OH: Merrill; Tindal, G., & Parker, P. (1991). Identifying measures for evaluating written expression. *Learning Disabilities Research and Practice, 6,* 211–219.

Table 5–4. Story element scale.

Element	A. Not Present	B. Present	C. Highly Developed
1. Main character			
2. Locale			
3. Time			
4. Starter event			
5. Goal			
6. Action			
7. Ending			
8. Reaction			
	A. ____ × 0 = O	B. __ × 1 = ____	C. __ × 2 = ____
TOTAL SCORE for Story Grammar:		B + C = _____	

Source: Information for Story Element Scale from Sawyer, R. J., Graham, S., & Harris, K. R. (1992). Direct teaching, strategy instruction, and strategy instruction with explicit self-regulation. Effects on the composition skills and self-efficacy of students with learning disabilities. *Journal of Educational Psychology, 84,* 340–352.

In addition to the story grammar scoring, a quality of writing score is also used. The quality of writing is rated on a scale of 1 to 7 that includes an overall evaluation of the writing sample as a whole. Sawyer et al. (1992) report that such holistic scoring includes traditional measures including aptness of word choice, grammar, sentence structure, organization, and imagination used to form a judgment about the overall quality of the written product. Mr. Johnson decides to use the maximum score available from the story grammar (16 points), the highest score available for the quality of writing scale (7 points), and another score for general appearance of the paper (2 points) to compile the total number of possible points per summary (25 points).

3. Probe frequently.

Each Wednesday and Friday the students are required to summarize the chapters they have just read, using the new strategy. The students have a total of 10 minutes to complete writing, but they mark what they've written at the end of 3 minutes for CBA scoring purposes. Mr. Johnson will score a minimum of two weekly work samples (what was written in 3 minutes) in written language for each student.

4. Load data using a graph format.

Each chapter summary is scored by the predetermined criteria of 25 points (see Figure 5-2). Initially, Mr. Johnson is scoring and graphing the written products himself, while concurrently training an instructional assistant in the process for availability of standardized and reliable scores across time. When the instructional assistant can score the written products with a high degree of accuracy, Mr. Johnson will spot check intermittently to ensure that reliability remains standard and high.

5. Yield to results — revisions and decisions.

At the end of the first 2 months of instruction with this process, it appears the students are making progress toward the objective, so Mr. Johnson plans to do several things. First, he plans to involve the students more in the feedback routine for them to be able to self-evaluate both their work and others' work. Second, he will include writing tasks from other content areas to assist with student integration of several curricular areas. Third, he will elicit suggestions from other content teachers about appropriate topics. Finally, more diverse and complicated writing assignments and tasks will now become the focus of instruction as the students move to the next objective or series of objectives in their curriculum.

Additionally, student involvement in setting self-selected goals for improving their written language is desirable, as is linking writing tasks to (or developing from) real-world applications. Students may be required to identify how writing is essential in community life, practice some writing exercises for the community as part of their assignment, and receive feedback and scoring as a generalization measure on their CBA graph. Linking the process of writing to the reasons for writing should be overtly addressed and elicited from students for them to realize that the exercises extend beyond school life.

INSTRUCTIONAL STRATEGIES

The focus on writing instruction in recent years overwhelmingly encourages the use the of both quantitative and qualitative aspects, as well as emphasis on the processes and strategies used when writing. Impor-

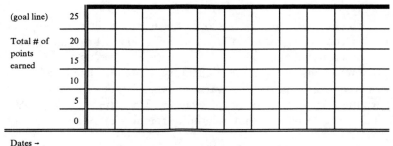

Objective: After reading a chapter from the literature book, the student will write at least two paragraphs that summarize the chapter so that a total of 25 points for story grammar, quality of writing, and general appearance are earned.

Breakdown of points:
        Story grammar possible points is **16** (see Table 5-4)
        Quality of writing scale is **1 to 7** (see page 92 for description)
        General appearance of the paper possible points is **2**

        Total possible points is **25**

Figure 5–2. Graph of written summaries of chapters.

tantly, several researchers have studied the impact of instructional approaches on heterogeneous groups of students that include students with mild and moderate disabilities (Montague et al., 1991; Zaragoza & Vaughn, 1992). Individual differences among students can effectively be monitored using a CBA system that incorporates (a) student's present level of performance, (b) direct instruction and strategy instruction teaching methods, (c) student involvement using goal-setting and self-management behaviors, and (d) progress toward writing across curriculum areas and generalization to environments outside of school settings.

Teachers can benefit from the current research on instruction and assessment of written language content for students with mild and moderate disabilities (see Table 5–5). Furthermore, they can contribute to that research by replicating methods in their classroom and using data from their CBA that document what works for their students.

Table 5-5. Examples of research in written language for students with mild and moderate disabilities.

Authors	Summary
Fuchs, Fuchs, Hamlett, & Allinder (1991a)	Teachers of students with mild and moderate disabilities in grades 3 to 9 who used skills analysis with curriculum-based measurement (long-term measure of CBA) in spelling elicited greater growth in their students.
MacArthur, Schwartz, & Graham (1991)	Elementary students with learning disabilities who were taught to use a reciprocal peer editing strategy made more revisions and produced papers of higher quality when revising their writing than students who used only a process approach.
Montague, Graves, & Leavell (1991)	When time and structure were provided for planning narrative compositions, junior high students with learning disabilities wrote quality, lengthy stories comparable to their peers.
Welch (1992)	A PLEASE (Pick, List, Evaluate, Activate, Supply, End) strategy was significantly more effective in developing the metacognitive abilities for paragraph writing of 6th graders with learning disabilities than traditional language arts instruction.
Zaragoza & Vaughn (1992)	Second grade students (including students with learning disabilities, low-achieving, and gifted) demonstrated significant growth in writing ability using a writing process instructional program.

SUMMARY

There are many different measurements that can be used by teachers to evaluate students' written products. A blend of various techniques may be appropriate for some teachers, but it is critical that teachers explicitly teach those chosen techniques and ensure students understand the rationale of the instructional lessons.

Student involvement in scoring and graphing written products can also be both motivating and USEFUL. Regardless of the type of measurement chosen by the teacher to depict student progress in written language, the CBA probe and graph should be *u*nderstood by all who will view the information, *s*ynthesize and communicate meaningful feedback to students and other personnel, *e*valuate critical objectives or the writing curriculum, *f*ill a void in the traditional assessment areas for written language, *u*sed frequently enough to provide good information, and be a direct *l*ink between assessment data and instruction.

CHAPTER 6

■

MATH

■ ADVANCE ORGANIZER ■

The purpose of this chapter is to describe curriculum-based assessments (CBAs) for competence and fluency in using computational skills and solving word problems. The influence of student proficiency in using strategies to solve problems is also incorporated, as well as functional curricula in mathematics containing meaningful and relevant problems.

C onsider the multitude of daily circumstances in which mathematical concepts, principles, and computations are used to predict
solutions, anticipate and solve problems, and distribute resources.

- Do I have enough lunch money to buy the large soda?
- If I give each of three friends a candy bar, how many will I have left
  over? Will I have enough left over to give to two more friends?
- The paper needs to be distributed so that each person in a class of
  24 students has two sheets. How many sheets do I need in all?

These are only a few examples of mathematics that people encounter in natural contexts — yet often the basis for teaching the solutions to
these examples are isolated from the computational skills necessary for
their answers (Cawley & Parmar, 1992). This chapter illustrates the use
of CBA and, although much of the research surrounding the use of CBA
with math has centered on computational skills, we propose the use of
CBAs to include both solving word problems that arise in real-world situations and student self-reporting of strategies they use in math. In
other words, the context for *why* we teach computations should be close
to the real-world applications, and *how* students use thinking skills to
solve problems can provide valuable insights for teachers and learners.

Although general education curricula at the elementary level quite
clearly is based on sequential movement through increasingly more difficult skill areas (e.g., division is preceded by addition, subtraction, and
multiplication competence), some educators question whether students
with disabilities must *master* these skills to progress in the math curricula (e.g., Horton, Lovitt, & White, 1992). If a student with math disabilities quite clearly has problems with memorizing computations, at
what point should the concept of using computations to solve problems
become the focus with the instructional shift moving from rote recall
of computations to application of those computations with the use of
a calculator?

At the secondary level, the math curricula typically is based on the
course a student is enrolled in: geometry, algebra, functional math. In
accordance with such national directives as the National Council for
Teachers of Mathematics (1989) more emphasis on the use of problem
solving skills has been called for. New curriculum and instructional standards are being developed for general education students (Szetela & Nicol, 1992). Regardless of the focus of the math curriculum, numerical
computations will remain a base for the measurement of mathematic
competence. This chapter provides several models for measuring computational skills and suggests an integration of problem solving and
computational skills. When long-term measures (i.e., covering approxi-

mately a year's amount of objectives) are used in research with students, the term CBA is often called curriculum-based measurement — or CBM. However, we do not distinguish between short- and long-term measurement terms; descriptions of CBA probes including behavioral objectives can denote whether a long-term or short-term objective is used.

Moreover, the impact on student performance when teachers instruct using sound educational practices is dramatic. Throughout this chapter, effective teaching methodologies are briefly described. Sources for more detailed descriptions of methodologies to assist educators in increasing and enhancing their pedagogical repertoire are included. For example, Mastropieri, Scruggs, and Shiah (1991) review math research for students with learning disabilities that includes methodologies such as (a) reinforcement and goal-setting, (b) specific strategies for computation and problem solving, (c) mnemonic strategies, (d) peer mediation, and (e) computer-assisted instruction. Teachers can refer to the original research descriptions of these procedures, which can be used in conjunction with CBA to experiment with various teaching methodologies while incorporating CBAs into instructional programs.

COMPUTATIONAL COMPETENCE

Fuchs, Fuchs, Hamlett, and Stecker (1990) investigated the effect of using computerized curriculum-based assessment (as a long-term measure) that included a skills analysis component. Students with mild and moderate disabilities in grades 2 through 8 were instructed with computational skills appropriate to their starting level of performance. Teachers were required to assess each student's math performance at least twice weekly. Each assessment contained 25 randomly selected math problems for variation or probe or assessment formats that sampled the computational skills specified for the corresponding functioning grade level for each student.

Although teachers in the control group also used individualized education plan (IEP) standards to set math goals for their students, the monitoring of student progress did not include either CBA, graphed performance, or systematic analysis of skills. Control group teachers reported that they used teacher-made math tests, observation of performance, and workbook or worksheet performance for their database. Ongoing support was provided to the teachers who implemented CBA. Results indicated that (a) correct digits is a more sensitive measure of student growth than only giving credit if the entire answer is correct, and (b) teachers who use graphed performance along with skills analysis plan more specific instructional programs *and* their students achieve better.

In a similar study by Fuchs, Fuchs, and Bishop (1992), teachers who used CBA set goals for students that relied more on ongoing systematic assessment, relied less on similarity of goals to other students or to the fit of the goal with the curriculum (i.e., convenience), and modified their students' goals more frequently, based on student performance.

Computer software programs can alleviate several of the time management concerns for teachers using CBA. Students need to be instructed in how to use the programs that compile and graph their performance daily (or several times during the week). However, there are cautions to total reliance on computer systems. If teachers do not conduct periodic inspection of student performance or do not conduct error analysis activities that lead to changes in instruction then the accumulation of computer data will not result in its intended outcome — that of assessing and making changes based on the data.

Fluency With Computations

Not only are students required to add, subtract, multiply, and divide with whole numbers, fractions, and decimals, but there is also emphasis on the speed with which these computations are performed. A basis for measuring both the acquisition and fluency of computational skills can be accomplished with CBAs that feature 1-minute timings of student's written answers to number problems. Although most often the entire answer is counted as correct or incorrect, a more sensitive measure is to count the number of correct digits within a 1-minute timing and to graph those data.

Fuchs, Fuchs, Hamlett, and Stecker (1990) suggest that the sample of items used in a CBA include the pool of problem types the student is expected to know by the end of the school year. In this way, more of a long-term measurement system can be used. Timings conducted twice each week should be sufficient to determine student progress toward the long-term goal.

Short-term measurement would include skills that students would be expected to master in a given period of time. For record-keeping purposes, the short-term objectives may be for a grading period, a unit of instruction, or as isolated skills within a unit of instruction.

A distinction is made in the literature between CBA which generally covers short-term objectives or single-skill areas, and CBM (curriculum-based measurement) which generally includes long-term objectives or multiple skill areas (Blankenship, 1985; Fuchs et al., 1990; Howell & Morehead, 1987). Teachers make the decision about which format to use and sometimes mix the use of short- or long-term measures with students. Skills can either be single skills or mixed skills (see Figures 6–1 and 6–2).

Cawley and Parmar (1992) suggest that school psychologists use CBA and incorporate other procedures to determine the stage of skill development, concept formation, and problem-solving abilities when determining the point to begin instruction with students with mild disabilities. This format can also be used by general and special education teachers in formulating instructional goals and objectives for a student's IEP. Curriculum modifications (such as allowing use of a calculator) may be appropriate, especially when a student has spent inordinate time (i.e., years) attempting to master the material modified. They suggest reduced focus on computations and increased focus on geometry, measurement, and problem-solving activities that can be applicable to functional life experiences.

Computations as a Prerequisite for Problem Solving?

Furthermore, Cawley and Parmar (1992) suggest that students with disabilities can be taught problem solving even before these students have mastered computational skills; contrary to popular opinion and tradition, these researchers suggest that the problem solving may even logically precede the introduction of computations. Their reasoning is that

$5 + 1 = $ _____	$6 + 3 = $ _____	$2 + 3 = $ _____ (3)
$7 + 2 = $ _____	$1 + 4 = $ _____	$9 + 0 = $ _____ (6)
$4 + 3 = $ _____	$5 + 3 = $ _____	$8 + 2 = $ _____ (9)

Figure 6–1. Probe measuring single skill mathematics (possible number correct per line).

$5 + 1 = $	$63 + 18 = $	$4 \times 2 = $	$37 - 8 = $
$7 + 9 = $	$12 + 6 = $	$8 + 15 = $	$25 + 45 = $
$17 - 9 = $			

Figure 6–2. Probe measuring mixed skill mathematics.

the ultimate goal of computation is its use in solving problems and that hands on activities can precede any instruction in computations.

Parmar and Cawley (1991) suggest that students be encouraged to develop their own practice mathematics materials. Furthermore, students who can develop a computational problem "such as the one shown in the example" thereby demonstrate that they understand critical aspects of the problem (see Figure 6–3).

Teachers may increase on-task behavior, promote active involvement in mathematics, and increase motivation for students who assist in the design of probe materials for CBA. However, teachers must also preview the materials to ensure that sufficient items and matches to the intended CBA objectives have been designated. Likewise, teachers may build on this by considering the development of similar problems, as a CBA in and of itself.

CBA can be both used and developed by students. For example, students are learning regrouping with multiplication and given the problem 257×43, are required to both find the correct answer and develop another problem similar to the one given. Through this, the teacher can assess computational competence as well as understanding of similar properties of this problem. A further extension would be for students to develop a word problem fitting a given computation.

Strategic Math Instruction and Measurement

Research by Mercer and Miller (1992) further substantiates the value of problem solving as well as strategic instruction that guides the students to not only arrive at a correct answer, but also to conduct self-correction and self-monitoring checks to ensure acquisition of accuracy and processing. Their work was initiated by a study of the concrete to representational (pictorial) to abstract sequence that is a mainstay of arithmetic textbook instruction, but is actually absent in many classrooms as well as another theory previously unsupported in research. However, further studies by these researchers do bear out the importance of moving from a concrete to pictorial to abstract approach with computational skills, and also emphasize how students can make the abstract pictorial by drawing a picture of word problems (see DRAW strategy in Table 6–1). Furthermore, the concept of having students develop their own word problems is part of the instructional program. One assessment involves 1-minute timings of math facts, each covering one or more computational skills, used to determine acquisition, fluency, and maintenance of the previously learned material.

In math, curriculum-based research appears overwhelmingly focused on acquisition of accuracy and fluency with computational facts

Solve this problem:	Make up another one like it:
5 + 1 =	
63 + 18 =	
4 × 2 =	
37 − 8 =	
7 + 9 =	
12 + 6 =	
8 + 15 =	
25 + 45 =	
17 − 9 =	

Figure 6–3. Probe measuring skill mathematics and requiring student to make up a problem like the one given.

Table 6–1. DRAW strategy.

Discover the sign.
Read the problem.
Answer, or draw and check.
Write the answer.

Source: From Mercer, C. D., & Miller, S. P. (1992). Teaching students with learning problems in math to acquire, understand, and apply basic math facts. *Remedial and Special Education, 13*(3), 19–35.

(see, for example, Fuchs et al., 1992; Fuchs et al., 1991). Ability to answer facts correctly is perceived to be highly correlated with the actual understanding of math concepts and principles, as well as necessary for solving word problems accurately.

The above sections have summarized various measurement and instructional activities in mathematics. Case studies follow that employ APPLY as a framework for developing and using CBAs. At the conclusion of each case study, several adaptations for the example case study are listed. Educators are encouraged to develop additional adaptations as necessary to ensure curriculum match.

Addition and Subtraction: Case Study

1. Analyze the curriculum.

Ms. Townsend is a special education teacher of elementary-aged students with learning disabilities. Ms. Townsend will begin the year with a review of basic addition and subtraction facts. Her instructional objective is: "Given a worksheet of addition and subtraction problems with regrouping, the students will write the correct answers at a rate of 48 correct digits per minute."

2. Prepare items to meet the curriculum objectives.

Based on the instructional objective, Ms. Townsend prepares several forms of worksheets that measure the specified computational skill. Each worksheet contains 25 problems up to the hundredths place, with regrouping involved. The random sampling of items ensures that no matter which form students use they will be completing a range of skills within the specified objective.

3. Probe frequently.

A work center (actually called a "Check-Up Station" in Ms. Townsend's class) is set up in an area of the classroom that contains (a) a timer that students can set for 1-minute intervals, (b) probe materials (the worksheets with the computations on them) in folders that students can easily identify and access, (c) a self-correction form for the probe material, (d) a folder that contains each student's graphs, (e) pencils, and (f) a chart with students' names, so that they can mark the dates they check-up on math computations. Each student is responsible for completing two math check-ups per week, and they may conduct their check-up anytime during their independent seatwork time.

4. Load data using a graph format.

Because Ms. Townsend has instructed her students with both scoring and graphing their information (which also coincides with a curriculum objective of graphing), the students are responsible for loading their data after each check-up session on their graph. Ms. Townsend is able to review the graphs on a weekly or biweekly basis to determine if goals have been met or instructional changes may be necessary.

5. Yield to results — revisions and decisions.

Ms. Townsend reviews progress for each student at least every 2 weeks by examining the graphs. Because she and the students have constructed goal lines and dates on each youngster's graph, she can visually compare goals with the actual line of student functioning. Furthermore, it is at this point that she is able to look at the students' actual worksheets and conduct error analysis of the types of mistakes made by individual students. Thus, she is able to formulate portions of the following week's lesson plans by reteaching specific error patterns. Moreover, for those students who have reached the instructional objective, she develops and assigns maintenance checks of previously learned objectives and prepares for instruction in new math objectives from the IEPs of those students.

PROBLEM SOLVING

Students with mild and moderate disabilities need to have understanding of computational skills, competence in correct and fluent computation of numbers, and a keen awareness of how manipulating numbers is a means for solving problems encountered in real-world situations. Some researchers recommend that a firm understanding of number manipulation precedes the computational and application components of math instruction. Although focus on answering problems correctly has been a major means of assessing math skills, national standards for math and some state assessment programs have encouraged more of a focus on how students arrive at the correct answer and the strategies students have in their repertoire for achieving the correct answer. In other words, credit for using a successful strategy is measured along with the correct answer.

Strategies for Solving Word Problems

Using a strategy to solve word problems involves a complex array of skills, knowledge, and ability to discern important information. Montague, Bos, and Doucette (1991) found that students with learning disabilities possess strategy knowledge that may be incomplete, insufficient, or inappropriately applied in solving math word problems. Consequently, students need to be taught strategies to be able to represent word problems, such as paraphrasing the content of the problem, visualizing the situation, imagining themselves in the problem, and drawing a picture of the problem. Students need to be instructed in strategies to develop a plan to find a solution and then perform the computation to solve a problem.

The following method for measuring competence in solving word problems can also address effective use of learning time at the beginning of a class period.

Word Problems: Case Study

1. Analyze the curriculum.

Mr. Huston is a teacher of students with mild and moderate disabilities in grades 4 through 6. Because there is a range of present levels of performance in his resource room class (that is, he manages instruction for students who are working toward mastery of curriculum objectives at their respective grade level, and each student is starting at a different point), mathematics is individualized for each student (shown in *underlined* portion of the behavioral objective). The instructional objective is: "Given a word problem that includes computations and reasoning with <u>addition and regrouping</u>, the student will earn 10 points for each problem solved according to the checklist of points earned."

2. Prepare items to meet the objectives.

Mr. Huston has developed a large sampling of word problems that include computational skills appropriate for his students (whose present level of performance ranges from 2nd to 4th grade, although they are chronologically in grades 4 to 6). On entering the classroom, students are instructed to select the word problem on a transparency for their group and solve the problem (a timesaver to prepare in advance to both relieve the teacher of writing problems on the board each assessment session and providing a reusable set of materials).

3. Probe frequently.

Two days each week, the transparencies provide "start up" activities that students are expected to complete at the beginning of class.

Mr. Huston collects the students' work at the end of 2 minutes (while he is taking attendance and conducting other class-keeping responsibilities).

Student work is scored on a 10-point scale, much like the evaluation criteria used by Montague, Bos, and Doucette (1991). The teacher's objective for each student can be individualized according to each youngster's instructional level in mathematics. One example of a behavioral objective is: "Given a word problem involving <u>fractional computations,</u> the student will write the correct answer by:

1. Writing how they got the answer by describing the strategy they used — 5 points possible,
2. Showing the computation itself on the paper — 3 points possible, and
3. Writing the correct answer — 2 points possible."

A total of 10 points is possible per word problem.

Because Mr. Huston uses word problem transparencies at the beginning of class at least 2 days a week, he has the option of using other types of problems to begin class the other days of the week. He orients students to math instruction by having a set task for them to complete when they enter the classroom and begins instructional periods by discussing the problems and how students solve their problems.

4. Load data using a graph format.

Students graph their performance on a 10-point scale, which represents the total number of possible points.

5. Yield to results — revisions and decisions.

Mr. Huston and his students are able to conduct error analysis of specific problem areas. For Mr. Huston, this helps him to target key reteaching areas for the class, a group within the class, or individuals. Furthermore, he may enlist support from students in the class to work with each other when reteaching is necessary.

Higher-Order Thinking Skills

Szetela and Nicol (1992) acknowledge that assessment of higher-level thinking skills in math creates new challenges for educators. Communication with students as a part of the assessment process requires that students communicate their thinking so that teachers can reliably assess students' efforts to solve problems. Furthermore, students often find it difficult to clearly communicate what they have done or what they thought in solving a problem. Methods for eliciting better communication of students' thinking is critical for more effective assessment.

Prototypes of CBA incorporating higher-level thinking skills and including a focus on strategies used to elicit the correct answer are in experimental stages. Teachers are encouraged to standardize their assessments, develop local school norms for general-population comparison with students in their school or district, and refine the CBAs for reliable and valid measurements.

Szetela and Nicol (1992) recommend several assessment formats that stimulate thinking and written communication for math problem solving. These can be adapted to verbal formats for students who have difficulty with writing. However, because written language is not the measured skill, a teacher can consider that a written response (a) encourages writing without giving penalty for incorrect mechanics of writing, (b) integrates writing with mathematics, and (c) provides practice for written expression. Such a format can involve:

- Presenting a problem with all the facts and conditions, but having the student write an appropriate question, solving the completed problem, and writing perceptions about the adequacy of the solution.
- Presenting a problem and a partial solution. Having students complete the solution.
- Presenting a problem with facts unrelated to the question. Having students comment about the quality of the problem or revising the problem to remove the incongruity.
- Having students explain how they would solve a given problem using only words, then solving the problem and constructing a similar problem.
- After students solve a problem, having them write a new problem with a different context but preserving the original problem structure.

It is critical, nonetheless, that a student who cannot communicate adequately (which can mean that the teacher cannot figure out what the student intends to convey in written language) should be provided alternative means of communicating their information. Some alternative means may include verbally stating information to the teacher or to another student, taping a response using a cassette recorder, or drawing a picture. At the same time that students should not be penalized for responding in a format that does not allow them to communicate what they know about the math problems, teachers should consider that requiring written formats can provide a forum for integrating skills across the curriculum as well as strengthening all skills. In some instances, multiple means of assessment (e.g., writing, telling, showing) can allow students to provide teachers with a more valid assessment of the math objectives being assessed. Each of these assessment methods can be easily written into a behavioral objective for a CBA that is used in conjunction with computational instruction.

Wiggins (1992) reports that Connecticut is experimenting with designs of mathematics assessment that both engage students in the evaluation process and assess their performance. The following are examples that could be used, or adapted, to represent items and formulate objectives for CBA.

- Given data on graphs, write a story that represents the data or graph.
- Given student work containing common errors, write a response to the student.
- Given equations or number facts, write a problem that the equations or facts could solve.
- Given consumer or job-related buying, selling, or measuring situations, solve a given problem.

CBA can be used to determine more effective teaching procedures and curriculum design features. For example, consider that students in a 10th grade class are receiving instruction on ratio and proportion word problems and the following scenario.

Ms. Scanlan decides to experiment with two instructional approaches after reading about Moore and Carnine's (1989) study that compared two curricula designed to teach ratio and proportion word problems. In this study, secondary students who qualified for special education or remedial services in math received either active teaching with basals or active teaching with curriculum design. Students in the active teaching with curriculum design group were taught to find the unknown value in a simple ratio word problem by being taught explicit strategies that could be used to solve many different problem types. These students performed higher on posttest results than the students who had received instruction that did not include explicit teaching of strategies for many different problem types. In the active teaching with curriculum design, students were required to demonstrate mastery of the steps and practiced applying the newly learned strategy until they demonstrated mastery in solving problems with that strategy.

Ms. Scanlan teaches one of her math classes using explicit strategy instruction for solving word problems. Another math class is taught using a direct instruction approach that does not incorporate explicit instruction in how to use strategies to solve problems. To measure the effectiveness of each group as well as individual student progress, she has developed a probe that includes a variety of ratio and word problems. Students in each class complete the probe at the beginning of class 3 days a week. Students are instructed to solve as many problems as they can in 2 minutes, and their work is scored on the basis of how they solve problems and correct answers given. Which instructional design is better? Which works faster? Which helps students more? These are all questions that can be answered by analyzing the results of CBA. Note examples of the probe in Figure 6–4.

Other methods of measuring student competence and proficiency with word problems, computations, and strategies used can be developed by teachers. The general education curricula, life skills curricula, and vocational curricula are three sources that can be used to determine starting and ending points. Long-term CBAs could encompass a range of skills the student would master in a year, with short-term CBAs possibly including skills likely to be taught during a grading period or a shorter unit of instruction. The following table presents a selection of mathematical assessment ideas for word problems. Teachers can use these suggestions to write behavioral objectives and develop items for CBAs (see Table 6–2).

Solve the problem $723 \times 8 = $ _____ . Show your work below.

When a person goes shopping for sale items and finds that 20% is off the original price, but the same item is priced differently at two stores, which store has the better sale price?

How did you get that answer?

Figure 6–4. Probe that contains computation, word problem, and strategy information.

Table 6-2. Suggestions for assessment items that measure word problems.

Researchers	Suggestion
Cawley & Parmar (1992)	Teacher reads a word problem from a script. Students generate the information set for the problem with objects or pictures.
Mercer & Miller (1992)	A sentence word problem including extraneous information is presented. The student crosses out the extraneous information, solves the problem, and writes the equation.
Wiggins (1992)	Given multiple or competing interpretations of given data, the student must justify each interpretation.
Szetela & Nicol (1992)	Teacher presents a problem without numerals. Students provide appropriate numerals, estimate answers, and solve the problem.

SUMMARY

Math concepts relate to many aspects of life. A teacher's challenge is to incorporate those life examples into the teaching of mathematics and to ensure that problem solving and higher order skills are measured. CBAs can be constructed to not only measure those skills, but to measure them during the instruction so that reteaching can occur. USEFUL (see Chapter 2) CBAs can lead to greater growth, understanding, and refinements of the teaching and learning process.

CHAPTER 7

■

SOCIAL STUDIES

CRAIG S. CUMMINGS

■ ADVANCE ORGANIZER ■

This chapter describes the development and implementation of curriculum-based assessments (CBAs) in social studies. Research indicates that students with mild and moderate disabilities are in need of alternative instructional and evaluative methodologies to be successful in content area classes. CBA is an alternative to standard assessment practices used in special education. Examples of CBAs that measure student performance in both social studies skills and knowledge acquisition are provided.

I n previous chapters, the use of CBA has been identified as an effective teaching behavior that can (a) provide formative and summative evaluation, (b) assist in educational planning, (c) help teachers to make data-based decisions about the efficacy of educational programs, and (d) increase the academic achievement of students with mild and moderate disabilities in the basic skill areas of reading, math, and written language. Much research supports this (Deno, 1985; Fuchs et al., 1984; Fuchs & Fuchs, 1985; Jenkins & Leicester, 1992; Mirko, Deno, Tindal, & Kuehnle, 1982).

Many students, including those with mild and moderate disabilities, frequently have difficulty mastering the goals and objectives of social studies curricula (Donahoe & Zigmond, 1990; Lovitt, 1989). These difficulties in acquiring knowledge and skills in social studies may be due to factors such as poor reading skills, poor memory skills, and/or a lack of organizational skills (Deshler, 1978; Lovitt, 1989; Swanson, 1987; Zigmond, Vallecorsa, & Reinhardt, 1980). Many social studies textbooks and instructional procedures contribute to students' difficulties because materials are often poorly written and lack a coherent conceptual framework (Anderson & Armbruster, 1981; Kinder & Bursuck, 1991; Lovitt, 1989). Whatever the cause, teachers need to utilize effective teaching behaviors to facilitate their delivery of social studies curricula. The use of CBA is one effective teaching behavior that can lead to improved student outcomes when implemented in social studies classes (Cummings, 1992).

Unfortunately, there has been little mention of CBA for social studies in CBA literature. A review of several textbooks (Howell & Morehead, 1987; Salvia & Hughes, 1990; Tindal & Marston, 1990) describing the development and implementation of CBA in various subject areas lacked information on the use of CBA in social studies. Idol, Nevin, and Paolucci-Whitcomb (1986) present a model for developing a science CBA that can be adapted to social studies. However, no data were reported that would verify the efficacy of this model for students who have mild and moderate disabilities or for students in general education.

THE NEED FOR ALTERNATIVE FORMS OF ASSESSMENT

Student Performance in Social Studies Suggests the Need for Change

Research describing the performance of students in social studies is limited when compared to the research on student performance in the basic skill areas (Kinder & Bursuck, 1991; Scruggs & Mastropieri, 1993). Proficiency in social studies is necessary, because (a) most states require that students earn two or more credits in the social sciences as a condition of high school graduation, and (b) a student's general fund of information would not be complete without some knowledge of history, civic responsibility, and geographical skills, facts, and concepts. General educators are usually responsible for the delivery of social studies instruction (Schultz, Carpenter, & Turnbull, 1991). When students with mild and moderate disabilities are involved in general education classes, special educators typically function as support personnel, advising and assisting the general classroom teacher in adapting instruction to meet the needs of students with disabilities. However, research seems to suggest that the social studies instruction currently conducted in general classroom environments is not meeting the needs of students (Donahoe & Zigmond, 1990; Kinder & Bursuck, 1991; Ravitch & Finn, 1987).

Ravitch and Finn (1987), in their analysis of the performance of high school students in general education on the first National Assessment for Educational Progress (NAEP) of American History, noted that the average student answered correctly only 54.5% of the items attempted. These authors express grave concern that students currently in high school lack even a basic knowledge of American history.

Donahoe and Zigmond (1990) analyzed the academic performance of urban, secondary students with learning disabilities (LD) who were placed into three general education classes: science, health, and social studies. Results indicated that 51% of the subjects failed social studies. Further analysis of the students' final grades showed that, in addition to the 51% who failed social studies, another 28% earned a grade of "D" (60–69% of the total number of points), indicating that 79% of the sample had below average grades in social studies. The data "raise doubts about the amount of learning that may have been occurring when learning-disabled students attended mainstream academic courses" (p. 26). Considering the large number of students with LD who earn below average grades in social studies, it appears that current instructional practices for secondary level students with mild and moderate disabilities in general education classes do not enhance student performance.

Traditional Assessment of Knowledge and Skills in Social Studies

The assessment of students' performance in social studies has traditionally been accomplished through the use of norm-referenced tests (NRTs). NRTs are tests that compare an individual's performance to that of his or her peers (Salvin & Ysseldyke, 1991). Most NRTs pay limited attention to the assessment of students' knowledge and skills in social studies. Achievement tests designed for use with general education populations such as the *Stanford Achievement Test,* 7th edition (Gardner, Rudman, Karlsen, & Merwin, 1982) and the *Iowa Test of Basic Skills* (Hieronymus, Hoover, & Lindquist, 1986) provide only limited space to the assessment of knowledge and skills in social studies. Similarly, tests frequently used for assessing students suspected of having a disability, such as the *Woodcock-Johnson Psychoeducational Battery-Revised* (Woodcock & Johnson, 1989), lack a thorough means of evaluating students' knowledge and skills in social studies. Most of these tests measure knowledge of a wide variety of social studies within a limited number of items. Considering the large number of social sciences and the limited number of questions used to ascertain knowledge acquisition, it is doubtful that these instruments are technically adequate measures of social studies knowledge and skill acquisition. In addition, NRTs are designed to discriminate among test takers. These tools do not provide the degree of specificity needed to determine instructional programming needs or to indicate precisely which skills have and have not been mastered.

In social studies classes, most evaluations of student achievement are conducted through teacher-made tests (Salvia & Ysseldyke, 1991). Teacher-made tests have several advantages over the use of traditional NRTs. First, teacher-made tests are curriculum-specific. Test items correspond directly to what has been taught in the classroom. Second, teacher-made tests are better able to discriminate small changes in pupil performance. Third, they allow teachers to provide both direct and indirect assessment of students' skills and knowledge. Unfortunately, these teacher-constructed instruments have been criticized for lacking careful item preparation (Thorndike & Hagen, 1978) and/or lack of technical adequacy (Tindal & Marston, 1990). Data reported by Nolet and Tindal (1993) suggest that "traditional measures of achievement in content classes may fail to align with the instruction that is actually delivered" (p. 46).

Teachers of social studies content must learn to develop their own assessment instruments, being certain to (a) use frequent formative evaluation procedures; (b) standardize their testing procedures so that the group of tests used to assess the same objectives are equivalent; and (c) develop tests that have content validity and reliability (Salvia & Ysseldyke, 1991). By doing so, they can ensure that student growth is measured accurately and that effective teaching methods are being used.

CURRENT TRENDS IN ASSESSMENT IN SOCIAL STUDIES

In addition to the traditional assessment techniques mentioned previously, many new approaches to assessment are currently being evaluated in the schools. Performance asessment, authentic assessment, and portfolio assessment are but a few of the methodologies currently being touted by teachers, curriculum specialists, and test makers as alternatives to traditional assessment.

Performance Assessment

Performance assessment may be defined as a type of evaluation requiring the student to complete or demonstrate the same behavior that the assessor desires to measure (Meyer, 1992). As such, it is a type of direct assessment.

In social studies, performance assessment of map skills may require students to locate cities on a map when given latitude and longitude coordinates. Students in a history class may be required to examine primary reference sources (e.g., tax records, census information) to describe groups of people being studied.

Well-constructed performance assessments usually require multiple iterations and revisions throughout test development. Poorly constructed performance assessments result in invalid measures of the targeted behavior(s) (Shavelson & Baxter, 1992).

Authentic Assessment

In authentic assessment, the student demonstrates the desired behavior in a real-life context. Although authentic assessments can be considered performance assessments, not all performance assessments are authentic. Authentic assessment is distinguished from performance assessment by the requirement that the response reflect a real-life situation (Meyer, 1992).

Authentic assessment in social studies might involve having a student make a presentation to a local governing council to effect some change in the way the local jurisdiction is being governed (e.g., adding a student representative to the local board of education). By learning how to get on the agenda for the council meeting and developing a presentation designed to convince politicians and citizens that the desired change is necessary, the student would demonstrate, in a real-life context, mastery of several skills associated with the curriculum of a class on civics or government.

In many cases, authentic assessment can be difficult to implement. Mainly, assessment quite naturally takes place in the contrived environment of the classroom. There are many practical barriers to implementing authentic assessment, particularly when the skills being measured are normally practiced outside the classroom.

Portfolio Assessment

Portfolio assessment involves the systematic collection of ongoing student work by both students and teachers. Portfolio assessment takes into consideration (a) the products that students develop, (b) the processes that students enlist, (c) the improvements achieved, (d) the effort put forth, and (e) how these features vary across a range of topics. In portfolio assessment, teachers and students work cooperatively to identify students' strengths and weaknesses. Evaluation is a collaborative process in which the student and the teacher share responsibility (Tierney, Carter, & Desai, 1991).

Portfolio assessment differs from traditional assessment in several important ways. First, portfolio assessment emphasizes self-assessment. Second, it includes evaluation of achievement, improvement, and effort. Third, portfolio assessment covers the wide range of students' work. A portfolio consists of the assignments that students complete in the classroom and at home. It is both curriculum-based and classroom-based, because it represents work consistent with curricular objectives and demonstrates mastery of skills that have been taught in the classroom.

In social studies, portfolio assessment might include the evaluation of written reports, quiz results, individual projects, student performance within a group (e.g., cooperation, adherence to the group's schedule of work completion), and videotaped oral presentations.

Portfolios can be used to check the validity of more formal assessment measures. They can also be used as a means of creating benchmarks of student performance across grade levels.

CURRICULUM-BASED ASSESSMENT IN SOCIAL STUDIES

The Rationale for Using CBA in Social Studies Classes

CBA is an appropriate means of evaluating student performance in social studies curricula because it (a) involves the use of frequent testing, (b) utilizes direct and repeated measures of students' knowledge and skills, (c) can be used as both a formative and summative evaluation procedure, (d) is sensitive to short-term growth, (e) is consistent with what is taught in the classroom, (f) provides valid data with which to make instructional decisions, and (g) employs a decision-making model that encourages professionals to move from a student-deficit orientation (Fuchs et al., 1984; Fuchs & Fuchs, 1986; Kaminsky, 1989). CBA helps teachers confront their instructional pedagogy and to change it when data indicate that changes are needed.

Inherent in the use of CBA methodology is the use of graphic displays to depict student performance. The use of graphic displays has proven to have a positive correlation with increased student achievement (Cummings, 1992). Fuchs and Fuchs (1986) note that when data were graphed, students' average achievement outcomes increased significantly. They explain their finding by suggesting that graphing allows teachers to analyze student performance more accurately and that graphs provide frequent performance feedback to students.

The use of graphing is commonly found in single-subject research methodology. As noted by Tucker (1985), CBA is one example of a measurement technique that uses single-subject methodology. Given the current emphasis in the professional literature toward adapting data-based instructional methods (Howell & Morehead, 1987; Marston, 1989; Marston & Magnusson, 1985; Tindal & Marston, 1990), CBA procedures facilitate this.

The use of graphs generated by CBA measurement procedures also promotes effective communication about student performance among parents, teachers, and students. Ysseldyke (1983) comments on the lack of communication that often exists when parents and professionals meet to discuss student performance. Because of the clarity and simplicity of the graphic images, the use of graphic displays of student progress facilitates the necessary communication between all parties (Deno, 1985). Even those untrained in the terminology and methodology used in education can understand that the upward slope of a data line indicates growth and that the steeper the slope, the more rapid the progress.

When implemented in combination with other effective teaching strategies (see Table 7–1), CBA can be used by teachers to help determine which instructional approaches are meeting the needs of students. If we are to begin effecting increased levels of student performance in social studies curricula, formative evaluation (CBA), which allows frequent insights into students' rates of knowledge and skill acquisition, is necessary. By employing the process, teachers can discard ineffective strategies and incorporate and expand effective methodologies. The result should be enhanced academic growth for all students.

The Nature of Social Studies Curricula

Social studies curricula typically spiral. In spiraling curricula, concepts that are covered are repeated over time, becoming increasingly difficult each time they are introduced. Spiraling curricula present special problems to teachers developing CBAs (Idol et al., 1986). Some of these problems include (a) the rapid pace of spiraling curricula, (b) the lack of sufficient practice provided before students are introduced to a subsequent concept, (c) the presence of gaps in the developmental sequence of

Table 7-1. Modifications in instructional delivery.

Method	Author(s)	Description
Summarize and record material on audiotape	Deshler & Graham (1980)	The teacher or assistant summarizes important information and reads it into a tape recorder. Student listens and reads with the tape.
Peer tutoring	Scruggs & Richter (1988) Jenkins & Jenkins (1987)	One student tutors another.
Use of reconstructive elaborations	Mastropieri & Scruggs (1989a)	Teachers and students construct visual prompts (pictures) that reconstruct meaning of difficult or unfamiliar words.
Mnemonic keyword method.	Mastropieri & Scruggs (1989b)	Mnemonic cues are developed to improve retention.
Use of structured study guides	Horton & Lovitt (1989)	Teachers develop study guides for student use while reading the textbook; ongoing questions are posed.
Activities-oriented approaches	Rutherford & Ahlgren (1990) Scruggs & Mastropieri (1993)	Hands-on processes are emphasized. Use of textbooks and reading deemphasized.

problem types, (d) the tendency of teachers to reorganize the sequence in which spiraled concepts are presented because of their own preferences, and (e) the frequency with which grade level curricula are overloaded with concepts, with mastery of all the concepts contained in a curriculum within a school year impossible. Although the problems inherent in spiraling curricula affect all types of learners, students with special needs are the most greatly affected. Special educators need to be sensitive to the unique demands of spiraling curricula and be prepared to make curricular adaptations when necessary to enhance successful learning of students with special needs. Often, in spiraling curricula, these adaptations may include limiting the number of concepts presented, teaching skills to generalization across settings, and requiring students to reach predetermined levels of mastery before proceeding to subsequent skills.

CURRICULUM-BASED ASSESSMENT IN SOCIAL STUDIES USING THE APPLY FRAMEWORK

This section illustrates the development of two CBAs in social studies. The first CBA is designed to assess student proficiency in using map skills in geography. The second CBA measures student mastery of key vocabulary in social studies across curricular units.

CBA of Map and Globe Skills: Case Study

In using the APPLY strategy to develop a CBA of map and globe skills, the first step is:

1. **Analyze** the curriculum.

In analyzing the curriculum, the textbook and the curriculum guide provided by the school system are inspected. To determine the skills being taught, check the table of contents, scope and sequence diagrams, chapter tests, and skills/knowledge reinforcement questions at the end of the chapters or unit of study. The curriculum guide usually has a listing of all the map and globe skills to be mastered. Sometimes this listing will include all skills being taught across the various units of study. Other times, it will be necessary to examine the objectives for each curricular unit to pull out the appropriate map and globe skills featured in each unit of study.

Ms. Johnson is a special education teacher, and Mr. Williams is a general education social studies teacher. Together, they are responsible for providing social studies instruction for Diane, a 7th grade student with learning disabilities. Diane has difficulty reading her textbook. Her reading difficulties encompass not only decoding unfamiliar multisyllabic words, but also comprehending important vocabulary presented in the text. However, Diane functions very well in class when information is presented in a multisensory format (visual and auditory) and textbook reading is not required. She also performs with greater success when important information is presented in "chunks," or short units of study, rather than long instructional units that might require a month or more to complete.

Following a thorough examination of the textbook for a world geography curriculum, Ms. Johnson and Mr. Williams selected the following objectives:

A. Identify on a globe, the poles, equator, continents, and oceans.
B. Correctly use cardinal and intermediate direction.
C. Demonstrate an understanding of latitude and longitude on globes and maps.
D. Locate places by letter/number coordinates or latitude and longitude.
E. Relate climate to latitude.
F. Relate Earth's rotation to time and Earth's revolution to the seasons.
G. Demonstrate understanding and correct usage of map scale.
H. Use a key to interpret colors and other map symbols.
 I. Correctly read and interpret a physical map.
 J. Correctly read and interpret a special purpose map.
K. Correctly read and interpret a general purpose map.
L. Correctly read and interpret an elevation map.
M. Identify the parts and direction of a river system.
N. Demonstrate an understanding of different map projections.
O. Make inferences from maps.
P. Compare and synthesize data from different maps.
Q. Compare and synthesize map data with data from other sources.

In the selected text (Harper & Stoltman, 1989), the map skills were introduced throughout the various sections of the text, rather than in one unit. Examination of other world geography texts (de Blij, Danzer, Hart, & Drummond, 1989; Sager, Helgren, & Israel, 1992) revealed a similar pattern of integrating map and globe skills throughout the content of a text.

An analysis of a 7th grade world geography curriculum guide (Howard County Public School System, 1991) revealed an organizational pattern differing from the district text. Whereas the textbook presented map and globe skills throughout, the curriculum guide provided a separate unit for instruction and review of map and globe reading skills. In addition, as in most spiral curricula, the map and globe skills were reinforced throughout the various curricular units by being included in the objectives of content-based lessons. The objectives for the text's geography skills unit included:

A. Identify the basic components of a map.
B. Identify cardinal and intermediate points on a map.
C. Define and use scale to determine distances on a map.

D. Describe the problems associated with transferring a globe to a flat surface.

E. Locate the equator, the prime meridian, hemispheres, continents, and oceans on maps and globes.

F. Define latitude and longitude and plot points using latitude and longitude.

G. Identify time zones in the United States, explain the International Date Line, and be able to compute time problems based on international travel.

H. Describe the relationship of hemispheres and Earth's rotation to the seasons.

I. Identify various types of maps and their purposes.

J. Describe the various climactic regions of the world.

Developing a CBA of a map and globe skills in a world geography curriculum presents some unique problems for Ms. Johnson and Mr. Williams. First, the skills as presented in the textbook are addressed throughout the curriculum sequence rather than in a separate unit. In the curriculum guide the skills are presented as a unit and then reinforced throughout other the curricular units. Second, the skills are too numerous to include all in a single probe. The curriculum guide includes a pretest measuring students' map and globe skills, but it is 5 pages in length, too long for a CBA probe, which should take but a few minutes to complete.

One way to deal with these problems is for Ms. Johnson and Mr. Williams to impose an organizational structure on these skills. By imposing an organizational structure, a CBA can then be developed for each of the organizational segments. For example, the objectives listed can be divided into four areas: reading and using globes, longitude and latitude, reading maps, and interpreting information provided by maps. Table 7-2 illustrates this organizational pattern. In addition, because Diane does better with information presented in "chunks," these four organizational segments allow Ms. Johnson and Mr. Williams to present the content in a way that will increase Diane's chances for success.

On the basis of the new organizational structure, Ms. Johnson and Mr. Williams develop the following objectives for Diane: (1) Given a globe and five probe questions from a geography unit on reading and using globes, Diane will write the correct answer with 80% accuracy within 2 minutes. (2) Given a classroom atlas and six questions from a geography unit on finding latitude and longitude, the student will write the correct answer with 100% accuracy within 3 minutes. (3) Given a classroom atlas and six questions from a geography unit on reading maps, Diane will write the correct answer with 100% accuracy within 3 minutes. (4) Given a classroom atlas and six questions from a geography unit on

Table 7-2. An organizational scheme for map and globe skills.

1. Reading and Using Globes
   Identify poles, equators, continents, oceans
   Use cardinal and intermediate direction
   Use and identify map projections
   Relate Earth's rotation to time and Earth's revolution to seasons

2. Latitude and Longitude
   Locate places by letter/number coordinates
   Locate places by latitude and longitude coordinates
   Relate climate to latitude

3. Reading Maps
   Understand and use map scale
   Use a key to interpret colors and other map symbols
   Read a physical map
   Read a general purpose map
   Read a special purpose map
   Read an elevation map

4. Interpreting Information Provided by Maps
   Make inferences from maps
   Compare and synthesize information from different maps
   Compare map data with other sources

interpreting information from maps, Diane will write the correct answer with 100% accuracy within 3 minutes.

Now that Ms. Johnson and Mr. Williams have analyzed and organized the curriculum, the items for each of the probes can be prepared and the probes for each of the four areas can be assembled.

2. Prepare items to match curriculum objectives.

When Ms. Johnson and Mr. Williams prepare the items for the probes used to measure Diane's performance in reading and using globes, they decide to use paper and pencil tasks, including drawings and/or color diagrams that must be correctly labeled.

The probes that measure Diane's skills in using latitude and longitude coordinates and in reading maps are designed differently. These probes make use of a classroom atlas. Each probe consists of several questions referenced to a particular map in the classroom atlas. Alternate forms of the map reading and latitude and longitude probes can then be developed based on the maps contained in the atlas. Appendix A contains a sample probe for measuring students' skills in reading maps and a sample probe for locating places using latitude and longitude coordinates.

When Ms. Johnson and Mr. Williams prepare items to match the curriculum objectives for the probes measuring Diane's skill in interpreting information provided by maps, they illustrate how CBA can be used to assess higher-order thinking skills. Here is an example of how CBA can do more than evaluate literal level skills of factual recognition and recall. Appendix A contains a probe for measuring skills in interpreting information from maps.

Once the items have been prepared and assembled, probes are administered on a frequent basis to assess Diane's rate of skill acquisition.

3. **Probe** frequently.

Ms. Johnson and Mr. Williams begin the daily class lessons with a brief drill administered to all students. Drills serve many purposes, including (a) activating prior learning and (b) providing students with structure and direction from the moment they enter class. CBA probes can be administered during such time as a drill-type activity. Data can be collected for all students and the results can be used not only to improve Diane's rate of skill acquisition, but to improve the performance of all students who demonstrate the need for performance improvement. Because the spiraling curriculum continually reinforces and reteaches these skills, the continuous drill-type administration throughout the year is not only appropriate, but fits the existing structure of the curriculum. Probes using this format can be administered 2 or 3 times a week without producing much additional work for teachers.

4. **Load** data using a graph format.

Reading and using graphs, tables, and charts is part of the geography curriculum. Having Diane graph her rate of skill acquisition reinforces this skill while providing motivation and an accurate picture of her ongoing progress. All students within the class can set performance goals and graph their individual progress toward those goals. Graphing and goal setting provide additional motivation for all students and often result in increased student achievement.

5. **Yield** to results — revisions and decisions.

Probes indicate to Ms. Johnson and Mr. Williams when their instructional methodologies need to be altered. The process also helps Diane identify personal areas of strength and weakness and indicates when reteaching may be necessary. When student growth is adequate, both student and teacher are rewarded.

During the first 3 weeks of probing, Diane exhibited significant improvement in her rate of skill acquisition in reading and interpretation of maps and globes. Ms. Johnson and Mr. Williams decided to include Diane's classmates in the CBA, as the others were also having difficulty acquiring the geography skills being taught. All students continued with the CBA until the required map and globe skills were mastered, as defined by the goals developed for each student.

Adaptations for Elementary Geography Curricula

Students in elementary grades often study specific geographical regions (e.g., Mexico, Canada, South America), concentrating on such skills as labeling countries, bodies of water, and landform regions on a blank map, and identifying some of the foods and simple foreign language vocabulary common to the regions under study. CBAs can be developed for measuring students' skill in labeling a blank map of the region under study. Students are given a blank outline map and a typed list of all areas to be labeled. They are given 2 or 3 minutes to fill in the blank map with the names of the countries, landform regions, and bodies of water. CBAs can also be developed to measure student mastery of basic foreign language vocabulary, using either a production-type or selection-type response format.

CBA of Key Vocabulary Across Curricular Units

In the next sample CBA, key vocabulary across curricular units of study is targeted. Most textbooks and curriculum guides contain vocabulary that is important throughout the curriculum. Frequently, vocabulary words are repeated within each chapter of the text and within each lesson and/or unit in the curriculum guide. The CBA developed below addresses vocabulary words crucial across curricular units.

1. Analyze the curriculum.

Mr. Martinez is a special education teacher. He is concerned about Angelo, one of his 6th grade students, who is having difficulty recalling the definitions of key vocabulary contained in the social studies curriculum. Angelo has difficulty remaining on-task during class and frequently makes unacceptable verbal comments that disrupt other students in his class. As a result of his inappropriate classroom behaviors, Angelo is not learning the key vocabulary at an acceptable rate. Mr. Martinez inspected the world geography text (Sager, Helgren, & Israel, 1992). His close inspection revealed that the following words were used frequently throughout the text.

atlas	confederation	equator
cash crop	geography	free enterprise

steppe	landform	peninsula
industrialization	socialism	precipitation
latitude	savanna	physical geography
nationalism	natural resource	rural
republic	weather	plains
economic geography	commonwealth	cultural
capitalism	continent	elevation
climate	democratic	economy
monarchy	export	humidity
culture	hemisphere	Judaism
ethnic group	Islam	longitude
globe	landlocked	Muslim
irrigation	urban	plateau

Because these words form the basis by which different geographic regions of the world are discussed, Angelo needs to know the meaning of these words if he is to comprehend the text. In addition, Mr. Martinez' inspection of the curriculum guide revealed that many of these words are identified as key vocabulary in the various lessons provided in the guide. Because of the frequency of their use, mastery of these words forms a core of knowledge crucial for Angelo's success in the world geography curriculum. Because of his difficulty in recalling the definitions of important vocabulary words, Mr. Martinez' objective for Angelo is: "Given 10 vocabulary words from the world geography curriculum, Angelo will select the correct definitions with 100% accuracy within 2 minutes." Mr. Martinez hopes that by administering CBA probes at the beginning of each class in a drill-type format, Angelo will respond positively to the additional classroom structure.

2. Prepare items to match curricular objectives.

Items for a probe measuring knowledge of vocabulary could follow either a selection-type or production-type format as discussed previously. Selection-type items sample lower-level comprehension skills, but are easier to score. Production-type responses sample more higher-level comprehension than selection-type items, but scoring the probes is more time-consuming.

There are 44 words in the list. A random sampling of 10 words per probe should provide a reliable index to student's overall mastery of the list, especially when probes are administered frequently. Although some variability from one probe to the next might be expected, the overall pattern of performance over time is more important. Even if every form of the probe contained all 44 words, there would be variability in Angelo's performance from one administration to the next. Using a "fishbowl" technique, Mr. Martinez prepares the probes. In the "fishbowl" technique, all

44 of the target words are written on pieces of paper and placed in a bowl, box, or hat. Items for the probes are chosen at random in groups of ten. A sample probe for the vocabulary listed above can be found in Appendix A.

3. Probe frequently.

By administering a probe such as this on a frequent basis, Mr. Martinez can get an accurate picture of Angelo's overall performance in the class. If Angelo cannot define these words, he cannot be expected to be successful in the course, as so much of what is discussed, read, and produced in class is contingent on his understanding and proper use of the words. Frequent administration not only provides motivation to Angelo, but allows Mr. Martinez to see specifically which words Angelo consistently answers incorrectly. In this way, Mr. Martinez is better able to adjust his ongoing instruction for Angelo's needs.

4. Load data using a graph format.

Mr. Martinez knows that reading and using graphs, tables, and charts is part of the geography curriculum. By having Angelo graph his rate of skill acquisition, Mr. Martinez reinforces this skill while providing constant review and reinforcement of the key vocabulary terms. Graphing also helps to increase Angelo's motivation and provides an accurate picture of his individual progress.

5. Yield to results — revisions and decisions.

By paying close attention to the vocabulary words that Angelo has not mastered, Mr. Martinez can be continually aware of the words that need reteaching and reinforcement. Frequent assessment of Angelo's knowledge in this area provides the teacher with constant feedback on those words that require further study.

CBA of Key Vocabulary in Elementary Social Studies Curricula

Curriculum guides typically contain a listing of all important vocabulary contained in the various units of study. Elementary school teachers can develop CBAs of key vocabulary across curricular units by examining the vocabulary listings found in a curriculum guide. Because content area social studies textbooks may not be used in the elementary grades, a curriculum guide should provide the most comprehensive listing of target vocabulary. Teachers can also use their own judgment in deciding which words students need to master in order to reach successful levels of performance.

IMPLEMENTING THE USEFUL FRAMEWORK WITH SOCIAL STUDIES CURRICULUM-BASED ASSESSMENTS

The following section reviews application of the **USEFUL** framework as a means for evaluating the CBAs.

The first step in the **USEFUL** strategy is:

1. Understood by others?

To ensure that the probes are simple to understand, teachers who develop CBAs should request feedback from content area teachers as well as from other special educators. In addition, student feedback should prove helpful.

2. Synthesize and communicate meaningful feedback?

Teachers should constantly evaluate whether the CBAs they develop provide data helpful in instructional programming. In addition, they should also consider if the students' results provide an accurate picture of progress through the curriculum by comparing the results of the CBA with other student products.

3. Evaluate critical objectives of the curriculum?

By seeking input from other general and special educators as to the appropriateness of a CBA, teachers can determine if the CBA is addressing the important objectives contained in the curriculum. Some skills, knowledge, or concepts may be interesting but not necessarily critical. CBAs should address critical elements of the curriculum.

4. Fill a present void/need within assessment?

CBA is a type of formative evaluation. That is, it evaluates ongoing student performance. Formative evaluation (CBA) is necessary for many reasons. The use of CBA helps students avoid failing summative measures (e.g., unit tests, final exams), as the process indicates when reteaching is needed. CBA also helps students to retain content previously mastered. Probes can be readministered on an intermittent basis after an instructional unit has ended. The occasional readministration of these probes helps students to retain content and skills already mastered. Special education teachers can use CBA data when writing students' individualized education plans (IEPs). Data generated from CBAs can be used to write IEP objectives and can be compared to more traditional measures of classroom performance, such as unit tests, homework assignments, and classwork.

5. Use frequently to maximize instructional time?

CBAs are most powerful when administered frequently. When teachers collect data that reflect students' ongoing progress. they ensure that valuable time is not wasted using ineffective methodologies. Frequent measurement also allows teachers to determine when students have attained mastery of the skills, knowledge, or concepts being measured, prompting the instructor to immediately advance to the next level of instruction. CBA also promotes students' involvement in their educational program and encourages them to take responsibility for their own learning.

6. Link assessment data to instruction.

Data provided by CBAs are only useful if teachers act on the information that the data supply. Teachers must be willing to use a variety of instructional approaches based on the documented needs of their students. In this way, students are given the greatest opportunity to be successful. Not all instructional approaches work with all students. Teachers must be aware of individual differences.

SUMMARY

Research indicates that students in both general and special education experience difficulties in meeting the requirements of social studies curricula (Donahoe & Zigmond, 1990; Scruggs & Mastropieri, 1993). CBA provides a means of direct and frequent assessment of students' performance based on the curriculum taught in the classroom. CBAs can be developed to measure factual knowledge, skills, concepts, and higher-order thinking. By using formative evaluation procedures (CBA), teachers can closely monitor the progress of students. When students are not making ongoing progress in meeting curricular goals and objectives, CBA indicates such lack of progress and the necessity for implementation of alternative instructional methodologies. When teachers are willing to vary their instructional procedures to meet the individual needs of students, both teachers and students benefit from the rewards resulting from successful teaching and learning.

CHAPTER 8

■

SCIENCE

CRAIG S. CUMMINGS

■ ADVANCE ORGANIZER ■

This chapter describes the development and
implementation of curriculum-based assessments (CBAs)
in science. Research indicates that students with mild
and moderate disabilities have difficulties when receiving
instruction in general education science classes and are
in need of alternative instructional and evaluative
techniques. CBA methodology can help general and
special educators who teach science to teach more
effectively. It can also help students to learn more
efficiently, with increased rates of skills acquisition.
Examples of CBAs that measure student performance in
science are provided.

S tudents with mild and moderate disabilities can have difficulty in meeting the goals and objectives of many science curricula. Their classroom performance is affected by such factors as poor reading skills, poor memory, and a lack of organizational skills (Deshler, 1978; Lovitt, 1989; Swanson, 1987; Zigmond, Vallecorsa, & Reinhardt, 1980).

Donahoe and Zigmond (1990) analyzed the academic performance of urban, secondary students with learning disabilities (LD) who were placed in three general education classes: science, health, and social studies. Results indicate that the performance of these students in science was poor. A grade of "D" or below was given to 69% of the students. Current instructional and evaluative techniques used in providing science instruction to secondary level students with mild and moderate disabilities in general education classes do not seem to increase student performance levels.

Carnine (1991) suggests that there are two primary reasons accounting for students' failure to learn. First, the motivational-developmental perspective of many curricula is inadequate for low-achieving students. The motivational-developmental perspective suggests that when teachers present developmentally appropriate experiences that motivate students, learning will occur. Students with mild and moderate disabilities may vary developmentally from their age-mates and are typically more difficult to motivate. Because of their difficulties with learning they may also have more limited educational experiences than peers without disabilities. As a result, the motivational-developmental perspective inherent in many curricula is often inappropriate for students with mild and moderate disabilities.

Second, science textbooks, similar to their social studies counterparts, contribute to the difficulties experienced by students with mild and moderate disabilities. Texts are often poorly written and lack a coherent conceptual framework. The rate at which new science vocabulary terms are introduced by textbooks can range from 300 per text in the 6th grade to over 3,000 in the 10th grade (Anderson & Armbruster, 1981; Lovitt, 1989; Woodward & Noell, 1991).

According to Carnine (1991), many texts teach for "exposure." These books present too many topics and are "indifferent to the conceptual coherence of the content and the pedagogical effectiveness of activities that are recommended therein" (p. 263). Therefore, many topics are merely mentioned and not really taught. Students with mild and moderate disabilities often need in-depth instruction and frequent drill and repetition to learn important new information. Few of the textbooks currently used in schools meet the needs of students with mild and moderate disabilities.

Several instructional methodologies have been proposed to remedy the current shortage of quality instruction for students with mild and moderate disabilities. Metacognitive instruction (Deshler & Schumaker, 1986) and metacognitive study strategies (Mastropieri, Scruggs, & Levin, & Levin, 1986) provide students with general methods for recalling and summarizing important information, learning mnemonic keywords, and using visual aids or concept diagrams.

Deshler, Schumaker, Lenz, and Ellis (1984) have proposed a "compensatory approach." In this methodology, more time is devoted to teaching fewer topics in depth. Materials are designed to provide students with an integrated understanding of a subject. Students learn important facts and concepts and to apply those facts and concepts to problems requiring higher-order thinking processes of synthesis, analysis, and evaluation.

Activities-oriented approaches (Rutherford & Ahlgren, 1990; Scruggs & Mastropieri, 1993) are similar to the "compensatory approach" by emphasizing depth of understanding rather than the scope of content coverage. In activities-oriented approaches, textbook reading and vocabulary demands are reduced and student-centered explorations are emphasized.

Mayer (1989) and Woodward and Noell (1991) advocate the use of conceptual models in the teaching of science. They argue that conceptual models, when paired with clear explanations, "help students think systematically and apply what they know to a range of transfer problems. Models also make explicit connections between concepts" (p. 278).

The effective teaching literature (Berliner, 1985; Englert, 1984) can also provide teachers with techniques in instruction and assessment that will maximize students' opportunities for success in the classroom. CBA methodology contains many of the characteristics associated with effective teaching. These include the use of (a) frequent testing and formative evaluation, (b) assessment instruments consistent with what is being taught in the classroom, and (c) valid data with which to make instructional decisions (Fuchs et al., 1984; Fuchs & Fuchs, 1986; Kaminsky, 1989).

Research supporting the use of CBA in improving student performance in science is scarce. Idol, Nevin, and Paolucci-Whitcomb (1986) present a framework for developing CBAs in science, but no data to support its efficacy with students who have mild or moderate disabilities. However, given the effectiveness of CBA in increasing rates of skill acquisition in basic skills (Deno, 1985; Fuchs et al., 1984) and in social studies (Cummings, 1992), it is reasonable to assume that CBA can also improve student performance in science.

CURRENT TRENDS IN ASSESSMENT IN SCIENCE

Performance assessment, authentic assessment, and portfolio assessment have been mentioned previously as alternatives to traditional assessment practices. The following section offers examples of how these types of assessments might be used in science class.

Performance Assessment

Performance assessment requires the student to complete or demonstrate the same behavior that the assessor desires to measure (Meyer, 1992). In using performance assessment to measure skills in science, the student might be required to perform a scientific experiment composed of one or more target procedures (e.g., measuring the boiling point of a liquid or conducting a distillation process). The student does not complete multiple choice or fill-in-the-blank questions on a written test as a measure of skill or knowledge acquisition.

Shavelson and Baxter (1992) provide cautions for teachers implementing performance assessment in science classrooms. They note that developing performance assessments is time-consuming and requires considerable scientific and technological expertise.

Authentic Assessment

In authentic assessment, the student demonstrates the desired behavior in a real-life context. In a science class, an authentic assessment could be conducted by having the teacher observe a student as the youngster completes a required laboratory experiment or procedure. In addition to evaluating the student's work habits and procedures, written lab reports can also be included in the overall evaluation.

Portfolio Assessment

Portfolio assessment is the systematic collection of ongoing student work by both students and teachers. Portfolio assessment considers (a) the products that students develop, (b) the processes that students enlist, (c) the improvements that they achieve, (d) the effort put forth, and (e) how these features vary across a range of topics. In science, portfolio assessment might include evaluation of lab reports, quiz results, individual projects, written reports explaining scientific principles or processes, and student performance within a group. In portfolio assessment, teachers and students work together to identify students' strengths and weaknesses. Evaluation is a collaborative process with the student and teacher sharing responsibility (Tierney et al., 1991).

CURRICULUM-BASED ASSESSMENT IN SCIENCE USING THE APPLY FRAMEWORK

In the following section the development of two CBAs in a science curriculum are described using the APPLY framework for their development.

CBA of a Life Sciences Unit: Case Study

In using the **APPLY** framework to develop a CBA of students' mastery of life science concepts and knowledge, the first step is:

1. Analyze the curriculum.

In analyzing the curriculum, the textbook as well as the curriculum guide provided by the school system are used. When examining the textbook, the table of contents, scope, and sequence diagrams, chapter tests, and skills/knowledge reinforcement questions at the end of the chapters or unit of study are used to determine the skills being taught. The curriculum guide usually has a listing of all the skills to be mastered. Sometimes this listing will include all skills being taught across the various units of study. Other times, it will be necessary to examine the objectives for each curricular unit for the year to pull out the appropriate concepts and knowledge featured in each unit of study.

Mr. Olsen is a special education teacher who is concerned about Andrea, a 13-year-old student with learning disabilities. Andrea is a quiet teenage girl who seldom participates in class and seems to lack confidence in her ability to succeed in science. Mr. Olsen knows that Andrea can be successful. As a means of increasing her motivation for learning and providing concrete proof that her skills are improving, Mr. Olsen decides to use CBA methodology. He meets with Andrea to explain the frequent testing that will take place and to provide her with the rationale for using it. He encourages Andrea to set a goal that is challenging but realistic, and assists her in drawing her graph and in writing her goal statement.

Following a thorough examination of the curriculum guide for one life sciences unit on one-celled organisms, Mr. Olsen selects the following objectives.

A. Discuss how one-celled organisms are grouped.
B. Classify one-celled organisms when given a list of each organism's anatomical characteristics.

C. List and/or discuss the characteristics of each group.

D. State evidence to support the argument that a virus is a living organism; do the same for a virus as a nonliving thing.

Next, Mr. Olsen inspects the textbook used for instruction of this unit. He finds similar objectives. However, the objectives presented by the text are more specific. Listed below are the objectives drawn from the textbook.

A. Describe the structure and shape of viruses.

B. Analyze whether or not viruses are alive.

C. Explain how viruses spread among people.

D. List examples of diseases caused by viruses.

E. List the properties of monerans.

F. Name the two phyla in the kingdom of monera.

G. List the major properties of cyanobacteria.

H. Explain how cyanobacteria can pollute a pond.

I. Name the three shapes of bacteria.

J. Describe the conditions in which bacteria can live.

K. List ways to prevent bacterial growth.

L. Explain how bacteria obtain energy.

M. Name five helpful and five harmful effects of bacteria.

N. Explain the importance of bacteria in the recycling of matter.

O. Compare protists with monerans, fungi, plants, and animals.

P. List three groups of protists.

Q. Define the characteristics of plantlike protists.

Clearly, the objectives provided by the two sources overlap. However, the objectives provided by the textbook are more specific. For example, C from the curriculum guide objective list is addressed by objectives A, E, and N from the textbook-based list. In this case, the text is more helpful when preparing items for the CBA being developed, because it allows for the construction of specific items whereas the curriculum guide is too broad to allow for the construction of specific test items.

Objectives provided by textbooks may not always be more specific than those provided by curriculum guides. The point is that by carefully analyzing both the curriculum guide and the textbook, Mr. Olsen could determine how best to proceed to step two of the APPLY strategy, in which test items are prepared to match curriculum objectives.

2. Prepare items to match curriculum objectives.

In preparing specific items that measure mastery of curricular objectives, there are several important points Mr. Olsen must consider.

First, because it is necessary to develop alternate forms of the CBA so that probes may be administered frequently, several items will need to be prepared for each objective. To ensure that the items have content validity, the objectives must be carefully written to employ behavioral descriptors, explicitly state the degree of proficiency, and note the evaluation criteria. Second, he must consider the types of responses desired. If selection-type responses are sufficient, using multiple choice, true-false, or matching formats is appropriate. If production-type responses are desired, short answer, diagramming/drawing, or actual performance of target procedures is necessary. Mr. Olsen must decide which format is appropriate. Clearly, CBAs with selection-type responses are easier to develop and administer. However, simplicity should not be the only factor considered when determining the type of format to be used. The critical factor is how well the format coincides with the individual needs of students.

Mr. Olsen must develop several items to measure each curricular objective. He makes a chart or table listing the objective and the items that will measure mastery of each objective. Figure 8-1 and 8-2 provide an example of how this can be done.

When a sufficient number of items have been prepared for each curricular objective, Mr. Olsen must assemble the probes (tests). The

---

Unit: One-Celled Organisms

Objective # __ : List diseases caused by viruses.

Item #1
Which of the following diseases are caused by viruses?
a) AIDS   b) hepatitis   c) tetanus

Item #2
Answer True or False.
_____ Polio is a disease caused by a virus.

Item #3
Which of the diseases below is **NOT** caused by a virus?
a) mumps   b) the common cold   c) food poisoning

Figure 8-1. Chart listing multiple item samples used to measure a single objective using selection-type responses.

Unit: One-Celled Organisms

Objective # ____: Name the three main shapes of bacteria.

Item #1

The three main shapes of bacteria are _____ , _____ ,
and _____ .

Item #2

In the space below, draw the three shapes of bacteria.

Item #3

The three main shapes of bacteria are:

a) spherical, rectangular, and square
b) chain-like, spherical, and rod-like
c) spherical, rod-like, and spiral

Item #4

What are the shapes of the three bacteria listed below?

cocci: _____ bacilli: _____ spirilla: _____

Figure 8-2. Multiple item samples used to measure a single objective, including both selection-type and production-type responses.

selection of items for each test form can be accomplished by several different methods, including the fishbowl technique in which items that represent each objective are cut into strips and placed in a "fishbowl," for selection by the students. It is also possible to select all #1 objective items for one test form, all #2 items for another, and so on.

Once multiple forms of the probe have been developed, Mr. Olsen makes multiple copies of each test form to have an ample supply of all probes on hand at all times. A sample probe for the unit on one-celled organisms is in Appendix A. When the probes are ready for administration, Mr. Olsen proceeds to step three of the APPLY strategy, which is to administer the probes frequently.

3. Probe frequently.

One of the many important characteristics of CBA is frequent assessment. Research (e.g., Cummings, 1992; Mirkin et al., 1982; Peckham & Roe, 1977) indicates that a frequent schedule of assessment increases both student motivation and student achievement.

Assessment schedules can vary for many reasons, but there are benchmarks for the frequency of assessment. Any CBA should begin with a pretest at the onset of instruction. The pretest results provide a baseline for measurement of student achievement. It also gives the teacher insights as to what students know before instruction. If students demonstrate mastery of certain content before instruction begins, the teacher can avoid spending valuable instructional time reinforcing skills already mastered and concentrate on the information that is unfamiliar to students.

Following pretest administration, a schedule for administering the CBA is developed. Probes should be administered to students a minimum of once a week. More frequent administration is desirable. Mr. Olsen decides to administer the probes to Andrea three times a week. By choosing a frequent schedule of administration, Mr. Olsen hopes to significantly increase Andrea's motivational level and skill acquisition rate.

With probe administration, Andrea's performance is depicted on a graph.

4. Load data using graph format.

The results of Andrea's performance are depicted on a line graph. The graph may be completed by the teacher, a classroom volunteer, or an instructional assistant. Students can also graph their own data as Mr. Olsen has decided to have Andrea do. She will keep her graph in the front of her science notebook. Not only should the graph show Andrea's progress over time but a line indicating Andrea's desired level of performance should be graphed. Therefore, her progress can be evaluated in terms of the outcome goal set. This goal has been established, based on conversation between Andrea and Mr. Olsen. Students develop ownership in their performance when they are included in goal-setting. The teacher's job is to provide guidance to the student, so that the goal chosen is neither too difficult nor too easily attained. Other elements that should be included on the graph include the goal statement and/or the objective being measured. Figure 8–3 shows a sample student graph for performance on the life sciences unit, one-celled organisms, described earlier.

5. Yield to results — revisions and decisions.

As data reflecting student progress are collected and graphically displayed, the resulting information describing Andrea's progress is used

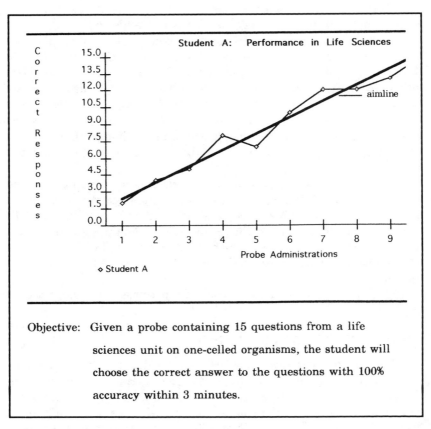

Figure 8–3. Sample student graph.

to make decisions about instructional programming and the appropriateness of the goal set during the previous step of the **APPLY** strategy. One of the main advantages of a formative evaluation procedure such as CBA is that it allows for appropriate changes in instructional methodologies.

In typical assessment procedures, teachers do not assess student mastery of skills, knowledge, or concepts until instruction is complete. In using CBA, teachers can determine if the instructional methodology they have chosen is leading to increased student outcomes during the instruction process, because assessment occurs frequently. If the instructional procedures chosen are not producing the desired effect, then instructional methodologies can be immediately changed to seek improved student outcomes. What must be emphasized is that a lack of student progress is not seen as a *student* deficit but as a *situation* deficit. When the desired rate of growth is not being obtained, it is the teacher's task to design alternate instructional methodologies to achieve the desired rate of student growth.

There are two basic decision-making models Mr. Olsen may employ when determining if his instructional methodologies are appropriate; the 3-day rule and constructing a line of best fit. In using the 3-day rule as a decision-making model, the guidelines are easy to follow. If Andrea's scores, as indicated by the progress line, are below her aimline on three consecutive days, Mr. Olsen must change his instructional methodology.

Constructing a line of best fit is a bit more complicated than using the 3-day rule, but the principle is the same. If, after constructing a line that bisects all available data points, the slope of this line of best fit is less than the slope of Andrea's aimline, then Mr. Olsen must change his instructional procedures (Kaminski, 1989). Figure 8–4 shows an example of a student graph in which performance has dropped below the goal line for 3 or more consecutive days (the 3-day rule), indicating the need for changes in the instructional procedures.

Mr. Olsen continuously administers the CBA throughout the curricular unit until Andrea meets her goal. Additionally, Mr. Olsen will administer the CBA at later dates to assess if Andrea has retained the skills and knowledge she has acquired over time.

Adaptations for Elementary Life Sciences Curricula

A key procedure in the **Analyze** step of the **APPLY** framework is to compare the curriculum guide and textbook being used for instruction. Considering that content area texts may not be used in elementary school, a careful review of the curriculum guide should be sufficient in this analysis. A life sciences curriculum for elementary school would contain different objectives. For example, many elementary school curricula include studying different classes of animals (mammals, reptiles, birds) or investigating the parts and functions of plants. Regardless of the exact components of the elementary life sciences curricula, the process for implementing the **APPLY** framework remains the same. The use of graphs to depict student performance is crucial in helping children visualize the growth that they are making in the curriculum.

CBA of Key Vocabulary in Life Science: A Case Study

A CBA can be developed to determine student mastery of key vocabulary for a given instructional unit or for an entire curriculum. In this

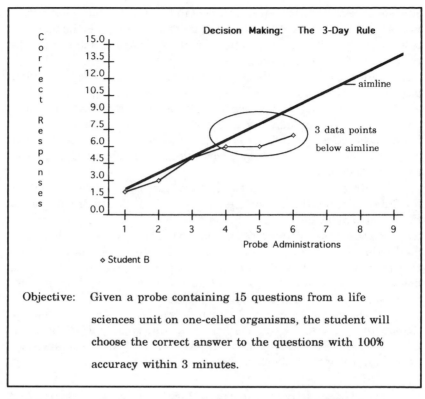

Figure 8–4. Use of the 3-day rule as a decision-making model.

instance, the steps for developing a CBA of key vocabulary for an instructional unit are described. The same procedures are used when developing a CBA for the vocabulary of an entire curriculum. Although the procedures for development are the same, there are two main differences. First, the various forms of a CBA for an entire curriculum contain samplings of vocabulary from across the various instructional units, with a CBA for one instructional unit containing all the key vocabulary for that unit. Second, a CBA for an entire curriculum is administered continuously for an entire academic year, with a CBA for an instructional unit administered until mastery of the content is achieved and periodically thereafter. Ms. Roberts is a science teacher who has several students with mild and moderate disabilities. Frank, Tommy, and Ruth are all having difficulty acquiring the vocabulary necessary for successful performance in science class. Ms. Roberts consults with Ms. Stoner, the special education teacher. Ms. Stoner suggests using CBA as a way of improving students' rates of vocabulary acquisition and providing direct and frequent assessment of students' progress. Ms. Stoner teaches Ms. Roberts how to develop a CBA that measures students' rates of vocabulary acquisition. Using the **APPLY** strategy, Ms. Roberts' first step is:

1. Analyze the curriculum.

The curriculum is analyzed by inspecting both the available curriculum guide and the appropriate textbook. Ms. Roberts' inspection of the curriculum guide reveals a listing of these key vocabulary words, with words common to the curriculum and textbook marked by asterisks:

protista	pseudopod	cell wall
amoeba	algae	protozoa
euglena	nucleus	food vacuole
vacuole	bacteria*	contractile
cell membrane	rotifer	cilia
monera*	flagellum*	DNA
paramecium	colony	

The textbook, which indicates key vocabulary for students with bold-faced type, indicates the following are key vocabulary for the one-celled organisms unit:

bacteria*	culture	fission
biotechnology	parasite	saprophyte
cyanobacteria	pasteurization	virus
flagellum*	mutualism	nutrients
moneran*	endospore	interferon

Obviously, there is not a great deal of commonality between the two lists. This presents a problem for both the students and for Ms. Roberts with vocabulary words in the curriculum guide that must be mastered, but likely not reinforced in the textbook. Ms. Roberts needs to assure that the words in the curriculum guide but not in the textbook are introduced and reinforced through classroom activities and discussion.

Ms. Roberts considers the curriculum guide the most important source in this instance, because it represents the standards against which her students' achievement is measured. The textbook supplements the curriculum guide and may be changed from one year to another. The curriculum, however, is less likely to be changed. Additionally, the text is chosen to support the curriculum — curriculum is not developed based on the textbook. Lack of congruency between curriculum guide and textbook occurs frequently in science classes. The situation must be addressed by Ms. Roberts in analyzing the curriculum. She should also have the flexibility to view both the requirements of the textbook and curriculum guide as a framework for what to expect of students, rather than as rigid guidelines. The needs of individual students are paramount, and if the needs of the individual conflict with the requirements of the text or the curriculum guide, the needs of the individual must have priority. Given the difficulty of some science vocabulary, Ms. Roberts may have to decide to limit the number of words for which she holds these students responsible. Although other students in the class may be responsible for mastering all the key vocabulary within the unit, Frank, Tommy, and Ruth may only be responsible for mastering 75% of the vocabulary terms. For this particular unit, Ms. Roberts and her students feel that mastering all the important vocabulary words is appropriate.

The next step in the **APPLY** strategy is to prepare items for the probes that will be administered to students.

2. Prepare items to match curriculum objectives.

When preparing items for a CBA of key vocabulary, Ms. Roberts must consider whether selection-type or production-type responses are desired. Selection-type responses represent the lowest level of thinking — factual recognition, as in multiple choice or matching items requiring only that students recognize the correct answer already supplied by the probe and underline or circle it. Ms. Roberts decides to use a selection-type format for Frank, Tommy, and Ruth. Selection format probes for vocabulary are easy to develop. A sample probe can be found in Appendix A.

Production-type responses require factual recall and the ability of students to express themselves in writing. This calls for a higher level of thinking than that required by selection-type responses. In designing a probe for vocabulary using production-type responses, only one probe needs to be developed. In this case, a limited-response or short-answer format would suffice and could be used repeatedly, because there is no danger of students memorizing answers based on letter choice (as in multiple choice questions). Appendix A contains an example of a production-type response probe for vocabulary.

Production-type responses can also be designed to require the use of higher-level thinking skills, such as justifying or making an inference.

Requiring students to demonstrate higher-order thinking is very important. In science, for example, students must constantly make predictions (hypotheses), evaluate the outcomes of experimental procedures, and assess the properties of unknown substances to identify them. Probes requiring higher-order thinking can be designed for assessing mastery of vocabulary and for evaluating mastery of content objectives exclusive of vocabulary. A probe that measures higher-order thinking skills and vocabulary knowledge is found in Appendix A.

Following the curriculum analysis, the items for the probe are assembled and steps 3, 4, and 5 of the **APPLY** strategy are applied. The procedures for completing these steps are the same as described in the chapter's example.

3. **Probe** frequently.

Probes should be administered a minimum of once a week, preferably more often. Administration of a probe should take no more than 5 minutes, preferably 2 or 3 minutes. A pretest (probe) should be given before instruction. When students have mastered the vocabulary, follow-up probes may be administered occasionally to determine if students are retaining the vocabulary and concepts. Ms. Roberts administers the probes to Frank, Tommy, and Ruth two times per week. She would like to administer the CBA more often, but on 3 days per week her students are involved in hands-on lab experiments. On these days, students need the entire 40-minute class period to complete the activities, so Ms. Roberts concludes that two times a week is appropriate for the probes.

4. **Load** data using a graph format.

In all cases, data reflecting students' performance should be graphically displayed. Student participation in graphing and goal setting provides ownership and increases motivation. Ms. Roberts displays her students' graphs on a bulletin board within a learning center that she has created for Frank, Tommy, and Ruth. These students use the learning center as a place to complete their CBAs. Ms. Roberts makes sure that the blank CBAs are waiting for the students as they enter the room. On the days that CBA is administered, students first graph their scores from the previously completed probe and then begin completing the current CBA. Ms. Roberts provides an egg timer for the students to adhere to the time limitations included in their goal statement. On completion of the CBA, the students take their regular seats within the classroom.

5. Yield to results — revisions and decisions.

Use of a decision-making model assures that Ms. Roberts does not continue to use ineffective instructional methodologies. When her students are not demonstrating an acceptable rate of progress, she changes her instructional approach. Not all students learn by the same methodologies and teachers must be prepared to vary their instructional pedagogy.

Adaptations for CBA of Key Vocabulary in Elementary Curriculum

Students in primary grades may not have developed the writing skills necessary to successfully complete a production-type probe for identifying key vocabulary. In this situation, selection-type probes are appropriate. Probes can be developed in which key vocabulary words are matched to pictures or drawings.

Students with appropriate writing skills should be presented with probes requiring production-type responses, whenever applicable. Allowing and encouraging students to use invented spellings when writing unfamiliar words can facilitate their responses in writing.

The development of cross-curricular teaching units enables students to read and comprehend target science vocabulary in the context of a language arts or math class. In this way, students are given additional opportunities to learn important vocabulary and to see the importance of these words in a broader perspective.

IMPLEMENTING THE USEFUL FRAMEWORK WITH SCIENCE CBAs

The following section reviews application of the **USEFUL** framework as a means for evaluating the CBAs that have been developed. Questions to ask are:

1. Understood by others?

When special and general educators collaborate to develop CBAs, they increase the chances that the resulting assessment instruments will be easily understood by and applicable for students using the tools, while remaining true to the curricula they represent. When Ms. Stoner and Ms. Roberts work together to develop the CBA evaluating students' knowledge of key vocabulary in a life sciences curriculum, both provide important input. Ms. Stoner, as the special educator, provides the expertise necessary to develop and implement the CBA. Ms. Roberts uses her content expertise in determining which words are crucial to students' understanding of the science curriculm and need to be included in the CBA probe.

2. Synthesize and communicate meaningful feedback?

Teachers should constantly evaluate if the data provided by the CBAs they develop are being used to make instructional programming decisions. Teachers must follow decision-making rules and be ready to change their instructional methodologies when necessary. In addition, they should also consider if students' results provide an accurate picture of progress through the curriculum by comparing the results of the CBA with other student products.

Ms. Roberts and Ms. Stoner pay careful attention to the results of the CBA. The graphs of students' progress indicate that Frank and Tommy are progressing at a rate that should enable them to reach their goal. The progress line on Ruth's graph indicates that her current rate of progress will not result in goal attainment. Therefore, Ms. Roberts and Ms. Stoner must change their methodology so that a more rapid rate of achievement can result.

3. Evaluate critical objectives of the curriculum?

By seeking input from science teachers, special educators can decide if the CBAs they develop are addressing the most important objectives contained in the curriculum. Because general education science teachers are content specialists, their input when developing CBAs is critical. As the content specialist, Ms. Roberts makes sure that only the most important vocabulary words are contained in the CBA.

4. Fill a present void/need within assessment?

Traditional assessment instruments such as norm-referenced tests provide data that compare an individual's performance to peer performance. CBA is a type of formative evaluation. It compares individual performance to a predetermined goal, evaluates the effectiveness of the teacher's instruction, and depicts students' rates of students's skill acquisition in an ongoing fashion. Norm-referenced measures and teacher-made quizzes and unit tests do not necessarily provide this type of helpful information.

Norm-referenced test scores for Tommy, Frank, and Ruth indicate that their performance in science is below age expectancy. However, the NRT data do not indicate exactly where instruction needs to begin, nor do the data provide information specifically related to the science curriculum being studied. CBA data provide this classroom-specific information that is necessary for teachers as they plan lessons and units of instruction.

Data generated from CBAs can be used to write IEP objectives and can be compared to more traditional measures of classroom performance, such as norm-referenced tests, unit tests, homework assignments, and classwork.

5. Use frequently to maximize instructional time?

CBAs are most powerful when administered frequently. Ms. Roberts and Ms. Stoner use the probes as a drill and reinforcement activity at the beginning of class. In this way, instructional time is maximized. The use of CBA as a drill and reinforcement activity encourages students to begin work promptly on entering the classroom and provides structure to the daily classroom routine.

6. Link assessment data to instruction?

Data provided by CBAs are only useful if teachers act on the information that the data supply. Ms. Stoner and Ms. Roberts keep a record of the various instructional approaches used with students. By analyzing these records, teachers may begin to see patterns developing indicating the most effective methodologies based on evidence of student preference and performance.

SUMMARY

Students in special education have difficulties in meeting requirements of science curricula (Donahoe & Zigmond, 1991; Scruggs & Mastropieri, 1993). To provide a learning environment more suited to the needs of students with mild and moderate disabilities, teachers can combine a variety of alternative instructional approaches (activities-oriented approach, compensatory approach, learning strategy instruction) with formative evaluation (CBA). When students are not making progress in meeting curricular goals and objectives, CBA indicates this lack of progress and the necessity of implementing alternative instructional methodologies. When general and special educators collaborate to develop CBAs, superior instruments can result by reflecting the combined expertise of the content specialist (the general education teacher) and the learning specialist (special education teacher). As the frequency of placing special education students into general education classrooms increases, these collaborative efforts become crucial. Such collaboration should improve instruction and assessment for all students.

CHAPTER 9

■

SCHOOL SURVIVAL
SKILLS AND
SOCIAL SKILLS

■ ADVANCE ORGANIZER ■

This chapter describes direct observation procedures linking school survival and social behaviors to practical, useful, and accountable interventions used in school settings. The importance of teacher-directed and explicit instruction in these behaviors is emphasized, and learner involvement and self-management systems are highlighted as key ingredients in promoting successful intervention programs using CBAs.

A daptive behavior assessments are useful for initial problem identification and eligibility decisions for students with mild and moderate disabilities, but there is a relative void of CBAs in this compared to academic areas (Cone, 1987; McAllister, 1991). However, there is a plethora of direct observation techniques and measurements of social and adaptive behaviors that are not specifically referred to in the literature as "CBA." These techniques and measurements explicitly use the principles of CBA for ongoing, frequent, and direct measurement of adaptive or social behaviors.

Although social and adaptive behaviors may be a primary concern for students referred to or placed in special education programs, reference to goals and objectives in these areas do not predominate on individualized education plans (IEPs). For example, Pray, Hall, and Markley (1992) reviewed IEPs of students with mental retardation, learning disabilities, and behavior disorders to rate the type and frequency of social skill objectives. The most frequently cited behaviors were task-related and classroom-compliance, with a limited range of social skill objectives present — even for students with behavioral disorders. Interpersonal IEP goals were either absent or not listed as a major educational emphasis, but academic and academic-related social behaviors were more likely to be found.

Although some students are placed into special education programs on a behavioral basis, other researchers have found similar results when studying the percentage of IEP goals and objectives that include social skills (McAllister, 1991; Myles & Simpson, 1989). If the initial assessments that qualified the student for special education services are clearly described using CBA direct-observation procedures, then educators should have documentation of the problem behavior in terms of both specific target behaviors for instruction and the acceptable range of peer behavior. By using CBA to observe both an identified student and a student whose behavior is acceptable, educators can develop peer-referenced systems to establish IEP goals and objectives. Cone (1987) quite aptly suggests that "a good rule to follow is to permit entry into a restrictive educational setting only after the exit patterns have been clearly marked" (p. 137).

Furthermore, most behaviors sparking general education teachers' initial concern fall within social interactions and work habits categories, not with academics (Fad & Ryser, 1993). Despite the need for more research and teacher training in the area of such behaviors, much can be done to construct valid and reliable CBAs in school survival and social skill areas. A wide variety of effective social skills training programs are available, many self-management techniques can be successfully taught for students to assume greater understanding and control for their behavior, and a variety of data sources can lead toward enhancing appropriate behaviors that are directly related to educational programming.

SCHOOL SURVIVAL SKILLS

School survival skills are those that enable a student to meet what might be conceptualized as nonacademic (yet extremely important) demands of general education environments, such as turning work in on time, following directions, and getting along with others. Although little of the CBA literature and research has focused on these aspects of schooling, there is a multitude of assessment and measurement devices that clearly fall within this curricular area. For example, much of the research in single-subject studies includes systematic assessment and intervention of behaviors defined as school survival skills and social skills. Texts by Alberto and Troutman (1990) and Burke (1992) are excellent resources for teachers who want practical information about applied behavior analysis techniques used in single-subject research. Many studies have documented the success of replacing inappropriate behaviors with acceptable behaviors using consistent and systematic behavior interventions and data collection techniques (see Table 9–1 for examples of data collection techniques that can be used for CBA).

Research findings include:

- De HaasWarner (1991) found positive results for preschoolers' on-task behavior using self-monitoring as the intervention.
- Salend and Meddaugh (1985) used a peer-mediated intervention to decrease obscene language of an 8th grade male classified as learning disabled.
- Prater, Hogan, and Miller (1992) improved on-task and academic skills of a 9th grade student with learning disabilities and behavior disorders by using visual prompts and self-monitoring.
- Hughes and Boyle (1991) increased on-task and task productivity behavior for elementary students with moderate mental retardation using a token economy and self-monitoring procedure.
- Walther and Beare (1991) used videotape feedback to increase the percentage of on-task behavior during seatwork time for a student with emotional or behavioral disorders.

Frequently it is the lack of school survival skills that begins to differentiate students with mild and moderate disabilities from their peers. General education teachers report that these abilities are among the most important in discussing the return of a student to a general education

Table 9–1. Data collection techniques and examples.

Term	Description	Example
Duration recording	Length of time between beginning and end of specific target behavior	Tally all amounts of time to get the **total number of minutes** student engages in inappropriate behavior; Use when there is concern about the length of time behavior lasts
Event recording	Each time a specific behavior occurs	**Total number of times** that student talks out in class without permission; Use when behavior occurs frequently
Interval recording	Divide length of time into time blocks and note if behavior routinely occurred during a specific time block	Student stops doing work for part of a 1-minute time block then off-task behavior is recorded for whole time block, yielding a **percentage of time** student is off-task; Use when any occurrence of the behavior during a time period is of concern; Sometimes used when teacher cannot record every instance of behavior, but can note if behavior occurs once during a given time span
Time sample recording	Divide length of time into time blocks and note if behavior occurs at the end of each time block	Student is observed only at the end of the time period for target behavior; Usually the **percentage of time** is noted on graph for behaviors; Teacher cannot record every occurrence of behavior, but time span is short and manageable enough to yield a reliable result
Latency recording	Note amount of time that elapses between teacher request and student compliance	Graph the **amount of time** it takes for a student to begin initiating a response
Continuous recording	Behaviors of target student and others in environment written down	Useful when conducting **functional analysis** and attempting to determine antecedent events (possible causes, provocations, preceding events), description of target behavior, and consequences following target behavior; Typically not for daily use on an ongoing basis, but extremely useful when determining where to start with CBA

classroom (Fad & Ryser, 1993). Social competence and ability to comply with standard classroom rules and expectations are sometimes more critical for mainstreaming decisions than academic proficiency (Epstein & Cullinan, 1987; Gresham, 1984). Special education instruction should include a clear and direct focus on increasing students' competence in school survival and social skill areas, so that the return to general education is not impeded by deficits in these areas. Consequently, special educators must utilize curricula and ongoing assessment that includes these behaviors.

Chalfant and Pysh (1989) consolidated results of five teacher assistance teams that convened to resolve troubling behaviors of students not yet referred to special education. The majority of troubling behaviors were nonacademic and related to work habits, classroom behavior, interpersonal behavior, and attention (see Table 9–2 for behaviors that may be targeted for CBA). Teachers reported behavior management and self-concept goals as most important initially in the problem resolution process, and that the goals shifted to academics after successful interventions were applied in behavior and image areas.

Table 9-2. Behaviors considered troublesome to teachers.

Work habits	Completing assignments on time; Working independently; Making an effort to do work; Following directions; Organizing work; Increasing the rate of work
Classroom behavior	Staying in one's seat; Not disturbing others; Following rules; Accepting responsibility for one's own actions
Interpersonal behavior	Making friends; Participating in groups; Exhibiting appropriate, mature interpersonal behavior; Sharing laughter and jokes; Expressing affection; Interacting with a variety of peers; Joining a group activity; Eye contact; Responding to approaches of others; Initiating conversations; Exhibiting polite verbal behaviors
Coping skills	Expressing anger appropriately; Coping when insulted; Accepting being bossed around in school; Avoiding arguments when provoked; Accepting correction or criticism
Attention	Attending behavior; Listening; Appropriate looking

Sources: Compiled from the following: Chalfant and Pysh, 1989; Fad and Ryser, 1993; Reiher, 1992; Stokes and Osnes, 1986.

CBA can be used to (a) initially measure a problem (for example, the amount of work completed on time, the number of directions not followed, how long it takes a student to begin work), (b) systematically apply an intervention (such as self-monitoring of work completed, contracting to turn in work on time, repeating directions to the teacher) while continuing to measure the identified target behavior, (c) analyze the effects of the intervention, and (d) continue or change the intervention, based on the graphed data. Furthermore, a successful intervention includes plans to eventually teach the student to maintain his or her own appropriate behavior (Stokes & Osnes, 1986). Training students to manage their own behavior has been a successful method to transfer the initial teacher-control of the intervention to student-control (for a review of 27 studies with special education students, see Webber, Scheuermann, McCall, & Coleman, 1993).

The importance of including general education teachers in the decision-making process is emphasized by Myles and Simpson (1992), who surveyed general education teachers about their willingness to accept students with learning disabilities and emotional or behavioral disorders in regular settings, contingent on appropriate mainstreaming decisions. No significant differences between acceptance of students with learning disabilities or emotional or behavioral disorders were found, in spite of the varying characteristics that distinguish these populations. Moreover, general educators stated that consultation with special educators and school psychologists as the most desirable types of collaboration they sought — with the specification that it is not the number of people available to consult with — but, rather the quality of the services available. The nature of the services can be improved qualitatively by including quantitative measures from CBA, training and assistance on implementation of an intervention (for example, behavior management, cooperative learning, peer tutoring), and team decision making based on the outcomes of the data gathered.

Furthermore, a therapeutic perspective on behavioral interventions suggests that the initial CBA target behavior for change (a) must be a behavior that is within the teacher's ability to change; (b) may be the most manageable, although not necessarily the most troublesome; and (c) can have spillover effects (Evans, 1985). In other words, the desired ending point, or goal, for the curriculum-based assessment must be realistic to achieve. A starting point for a CBA can also have positive effects on other types of behavior not measured with the CBA. When one goal is achieved then the student, teacher, and others involved in the CBA process can target a more ambitious goal. Table 9–3 lists several examples of school survival skills, descriptions of behaviors, and possible assessment approaches that can be used as the CBA.

Table 9–3. Examples of curriculum-based assessments for school survival skills.

School Survival Skill	Behavior	Assessment
Complete homework assignments	Complete and turn in homework assignments on time	Number of completed assignments turned in on time
Using school work time efficiently	Beginning and completing assigned work during the school day	Number of minutes it takes a student to begin work after teacher directions; Work turned in by the end of the period
Organizing materials	Uses folders, notebooks or other organizers for storage and retrieval	Checklist used to periodically assess organizational practices throughout the school day
Following directions	Begins to follow directions within 1 minute	Amount of time it takes for student to begin following directions
Raising hand to participate in class discussions	Participates in class discussions only after raising hand and being called on by the teacher	Number of times student participates by raising hand and being called on by the teacher
On-task	Completes assignments with a specified amount of accuracy	Percentage of work completed within allotted time and with a predetermined accuracy rate

The following case study illustrates how a teacher deals with the development of school survival skills through using self-management techniques with a student.

Self-Management: Case Study

1. Analyze the curriculum.

The curriculum for school survival skills covers student behaviors enabling a student to experience academic success in school, and also applies to those behaviors enabling a student to qualify for vocational success. Ms. Solomon is a special education teacher who is particularly concerned about Donald, a 3rd grade student with learning disabilities and emotional adjustment problems. Donald seldom begins his work without a long delay, and, subsequently, seldom turns in completed work on time. Donald seems capable of completing the work accurately and, therefore, he is being considered by the school committee for return to general education classrooms. Ms. Solomon is well aware that Donald's inability to work independently could hamper his success in general education. Her objective for Donald is: "Given an assignment, Donald will turn in the completed assignment (1) within 30 minutes of receiving it and (2) with at least 90% of the work completed accurately."

2. Prepare items to meet the curriculum objective.

A self-management checklist is developed by Ms. Solomon and Donald. The checklist contains four columns and enough rows for each of five assignments given during the day (see Table 9–4). Ms. Solomon completes the "Assignment" column at the beginning of each day. Donald writes down the time he begins and finishes each assignment and makes a checkmark in the appropriate column when he is finished. For "Percentage correct," Donald can use self-correcting materials to score his own work, a peer can score the work, or Ms. Solomon can score Donald's work.

3. Probe frequently.

While the teacher is collecting data on Donald's behavior, Donald is actually involved in the process throughout the day, with results tallied at the end of each day, providing a number of points earned. The total number of points earned are graphed by Donald at the end of each day (see Figure 9–1).

4. Load data using graph format.

The visual representation gives both Ms. Solomon and Donald a clear picture of how much work he is doing in her class. Ms. Solomon plans to have Donald use a similar system in the general education classroom.

5. Yield to results — revisions and decisions.

Table 9-4. Self-management checklist for Donald.

Assignment	Time Began and Time Finished	Percentage Correct	Check When Completed
1. page 53, math book	9:15 to 9:35	92%	
2. reading questions	10:05 to 10:22	8/10 answered correctly	
3. report outline, social studies	11:13 to 11:45	4/5 outline requirements met	
4. spelling sentences written	1:10 to 1:24	12/12 spelling words used in sentences	
5. homework assignment written down and materials gathered to take home	2:45 to 2:50	3/3 homework assignments written in notebook and all materials needed are in book bag	

Total number of assignments completed with minimum of 90% accuracy:

After 3 weeks, there is a marked improvement in the amount of work Donald is completing and the amount of time it is taking him to complete this work. Ms. Solomon decides to continue with the self-management checklist but to fade her involvement, continue to verbally reinforce Donald for working independently, and to encourage Donald to use the checklist "when he needs it" for him to see the relationship between his responsibility for his work output with and without the graph. Ms. Solomon is hopeful that his work output will maintain his present level of performance. If not, she will conference with Donald and reinstate the self-management checklist.

Variations of APPLY With Donald

For young children, using stickers or smiley faces may be used instead of a checkmark — and can also be the reinforcement itself. Token economies in which youngsters earn points for special privileges or rewards may be necessary initially, but Ms. Solomon wants to fade to more natu-

Objective: Given an assignment, the student will turn in the completed assignment (1) within 30 minutes of receiving it and (2) with at least 90% of the work completed accurately.

Scenario for this graph: The student earns 10 points for turning in the work within 30 minutes of receiving it, and then is eligible for 10 additional points if 90% of the work is correct. The graph is set up for 5 assignments per day, which should be consistent (possible number of points per day is 100). If the number of assignments change each day, then the teacher should change the graph to "percentage of possible points earned."

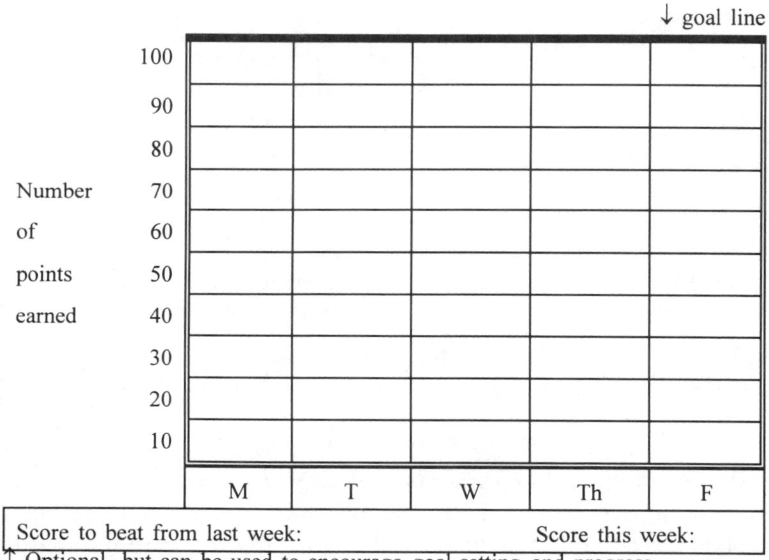

↓ goal line

	M	T	W	Th	F
100					
90					
80					
70					
60					
50					
40					
30					
20					
10					

Number of points earned

Score to beat from last week: Score this week:

↑ Optional, but can be used to encourage goal-setting and progress.

Note: Student can either earn points for both (1) and (2) of the objective, or the student can earn points for (1) separate from (2). Teacher judgment and student involvement can be the determinants of the chosen point system. The criteria for points earned should be discussed well with the student.

Figure 9–1. Graph for points earned through self-management system.

ral consequences as soon as Donald is successfully completing all assignments. For Donald to realize that he is responsible for his appropriate behavior, discussions between him and his teacher include prompts for him to talk about his thoughts and feelings when he has successfully accomplished his tasks. Donald can be explicitly involved in goal-setting with self-management by (a) self-targeting when he will complete assignments, (b) informing the teacher when he no longer needs to fill out the checklist after every assignment, but that he can wait until the end of the day, and (c) suggesting his other behaviors that would be appropriate for "checklist reminders."

Foley and Epstein (1993) explored the value of a School Survival Skill curriculum in developing and improving the school survival skills of junior high and middle school students with emotional or behavioral disorders. They found significant differences with task-oriented and compliance behaviors achieved after instruction with this curriculum, but that organizational skills, task completion, independence, and school rules did not achieve the same success. Foley and Epstein recommended that school survival skill curricula for students with emotional or behavioral disorders may need (a) more direct instruction in strategies for these skills, (b) more direct instruction with basic academic skills, and (c) frequent and direct measures of these skills used in conjunction with the survival skill instruction. Clearly, this last item indicates the need for CBA that monitors the effectiveness of such curricula.

SOCIAL SKILLS

Stokes and Osnes (1986) suggest that definitions of social behaviors necessarily implies those behaviors that are displayed both in the presence of and in the context of interactions with others. Consequently, when social behaviors are targeted for assessment and change, the environmental and situational events in which the target behavior occurs must be determined and included in the assessment process. Several researchers suggest that a "functional analysis" of a target behavior is needed (O'Neill, Horner, Albin, Storey, & Sprague, 1990) to more accurately identify critical variables that should become a part of the intervention process. In other words, it is important to determine the cause and effect aspects of the target behavior to determine if there are variables other than the student that need to be changed or influenced.

Germann and Tindal (1985) reported that observation systems for social behaviors involve more time and personnel than for academic behaviors and, therefore, such measurement may occur on a less frequent basis. However, training teachers and instructional assistants in data collection procedures (such as time sampling, event recording, permanent product scoring), involving other personnel (for example, the school psychologist may conduct weekly assessments by observing the student and interviewing the teacher), and training the student to self-monitor behaviors may alleviate the time and personnel constraints, also enhancing the effectiveness of the program through collaboration among adults and the student.

The importance of observation systems that can be used as CBAs is emphasized by Coleman, Wheeler, and Webber (1993) in their review of interpersonal problem-solving training. They found that social validity (acceptability of interventions to consumers, i.e., students) increased when behavior observations were added to measures of interpersonal problem-solving training. Moreover, it was found to be important to determine whether or not students who received interpersonal problem-solving training were repertoire deficit (did not know problem-solving strategies) or performance deficit (did not know how to use problem-solving strategies). Furthermore, students did not automatically transfer the training to other settings and situations unless specifically instructed in generalization methods.

Three types of observation scenarios can be used to help ensure generalization, or transfer, of social skills. First, students may be observed during role-play situations in which they are learning the social skill (for example, "accepting criticism"). Next, students may be observed in contrived, or surprise, situations to determine if learned social behaviors transfer to an unreal situation. Finally, students must be observed in natural settings to ensure that the target skills generalize. Teachers who teach students social skills only in classroom settings without giving attention to other social skills settings or situations will find it difficult, if not impossible, to determine if there is generalization to other environments. Moreover, the teacher feedback about how students perform social skills in real situations involving both the students themselves and classmates is a critical part of the instructional process.

Teaching students how to become more socially adept often requires teaching step-by-step methods for recognizing the inappropriateness of their behaviors, motivating students to use more acceptable responses, and teaching students strategies for performing in a different manner. The following case study relates how one teacher teaches coping skills to a student.

Coping Skills: Case Study

1. Analyze the curriculum.

Beatrice is a student in a 4th grade class for students with emotional or behavioral disorders. Ms. Reynolds, her teacher, says that Beatrice needs to learn to ask for help instead of aggressively acting out, becoming frustrated, and disrupting other students with tantrums. The IEP objective written for Beatrice states that: "Given the opportunity to request help, Beatrice will ask for help by raising her hand and asking for help in a friendly way." Another version of an IEP objective could read: "Given an instructional day, Beatrice will display zero episodes of tantrums for 5 consecutive days."

2. Prepare items to meet the objective.

Because Beatrice needs to learn how to ask for help in a positive manner without becoming frustrated, the actual behaviors involved in asking for help are the items that become the probe for this objective. Ms. Reynolds is using *The Elementary School Child: A Guide for Teaching Prosocial Skills* (McGinnis & Goldstein, 1984), which lists the following process for this objective.

First, Beatrice must ask herself "Can I do this alone?" If she cannot, then she should raise her hand. When the teacher is occupied with another student, Beatrice is instructed to self-talk about waiting quietly ("I know I can wait without talking"). Finally, she should ask for help in a friendly way when the teacher acknowledges her raised hand.

3. Probe frequently.

Ms. Reynolds instructs Beatrice in the appropriate behaviors for asking for help in conjunction with social studies, or citizenship, lessons. Because the most frequent acting out behaviors happen during the math lesson (which may also have implications for examining Beatrice's instructional level in math to ensure it is appropriate), Ms. Reynolds has collected data during the 30 minutes before social skill instruction. In this way, Ms. Reynolds hopes to determine if any changes are made in Beatrice's behavior because she has an opportunity to learn them, practice them, and discuss them at a time other than during math. Ms. Reynolds collects data each day on the number of tantrums Beatrice has during math.

4. Load data using a graph format.

The number of tantrums Beatrice exhibits during math time are recorded on a graph that Ms. Reynolds keeps. Concurrently, Ms. Reynolds is also completing a checklist of Beatrice's appropriate social skill behaviors during role-play situations at other times of the day. Ms. Reynolds intends to share the results of the checklist and the number of tantrums with Beatrice so that the youngster becomes more aware of the correlation between the behaviors of using the checklist and having fewer frustrating episodes.

5. Yield to results — revisions and decisions.

The more Ms. Reynolds can get Beatrice to display appropriate social skill behaviors, the less frustrated Beatrice is likely to become. Beatrice is given a checklist of the "asking for help" behaviors for her use during math time. Additionally, a favored peer has been enlisted to prompt Beatrice to use her checklist.

Peer-mediated interventions (such as group reinforcement, peer modeling and role play, peer prompting and reinforcement, and peer initiation) have been successfully used to increase social skills of students with disabilities. However, studies that have employed peer-mediation to promote social skills of students with emotional or behavioral disorders (see Mathur & Rutherford, 1991, for a review) and preschool children with disabilities (Hundert & Houghton, 1992) have relied on teacher supervision and prompting. That is, training peers — or students — alone is not sufficient. Furthermore, training must include specific plans to extend social skills learned within a school program to other natural settings.

Social acceptance of students with learning disabilities in a full-time integrated program was examined by Juvonen and Bear (1992). Social status, friendships, and self-perceptions of social acceptance were examined for students who were receiving all of their instruction in a program taught by a special education and a general education teacher in a model called Team Approach to Mastery. The results of their study showed that children with learning disabilities are well socially integrated in Team Approach to Mastery classrooms. But Juvonen and Bear (1992) caution that their results may not generalize to classrooms without adequate support. This study further emphasizes the critical role that social factors have for students with and without disabilities.

Social Competence

Coleman and Minnett (1992) used several rating systems to compare the social competence of students with learning disabilities with their peers who were not labeled with a disability. The systems employed included academic grades, teacher perceptions, peer perceptions, self-perceptions, social network outside of school, and direct observation of social interactions. Because the results of their study found that social differences were linked more to peer status, regardless of disability, Coleman and Minnett recommended that social skills training programs (refer to Elksnin, 1989, for a review of social skill training programs) that have been well-developed for special education students would also benefit general education students. In other words, students with and without disabilities would profit from systematic instruction to increase their social skills and self-concept.

Reiher (1992) found that students who were assessed and placed in programs for students with behavioral disorders contained few social-emotional goals on their IEPs. He said it was possible that people who write IEPs might believe social/emotional instruction to be too difficult to provide, thereby focusing more on instruction aimed at behavioral (for example, on-task) and academic deficits. Reiher concludes that the procedures used in the evaluation process need to easily translate to IEP goals and objectives. That is, when social emotional concerns are the basis for placement in special education, then the personnel who have conducted the evaluation should (a) use systematic behavioral observation and measurement, (b) translate these assessment results into IEP goals and objectives, and (c) monitor the implementation and effects of chosen social-emotional instruction. Moreover, the use of systematic behavioral observation and measurement is in keeping with CBA principles of having observable and frequent measurement that can be used to evaluate the effectiveness of instruction.

McAllister (1991) suggests that effective curriculum-based behavioral instruction and assessment include the following:

- The social instructional program be direct and ongoing and eventually blended with academic curriculum for more durable outcomes.
- A proactive, versus preventive or reactive, approach be used through direct teaching of social and behavioral skills.
- Special educators use their existing instructional methods for teaching social and behavioral skills.
- A comprehensive approach to developing CBAs be used to develop multiple skills (e.g., peer and adult interactions, compliance, self-regulation).
- A CBA approach includes interventions directed at or using peers, environmental modifications, or other appropriate interventions. That is, interventions may not be solely aimed at the target student, but also address ecological variables as well.

SUMMARY

General education and special education teachers are well aware of the troublesome behaviors displayed by students with mild and moderate disabilities, as well as by students who do not have an identified disability.

The suggestions for instruction and measurement in this chapter provide interventions *and* assessment methods that can document desirable changes or can inform teachers when another intervention should be tried. USEFUL CBAs in school survival skills and social skill areas can enhance both the learning and social environment of classrooms.

REFERENCES

Alberto, P. A., & Troutman, A. C. (1990). *Applied behavior analysis for teachers* (3rd ed.). Columbus, OH: Merrill Publishing Company.

Allan, K. K., & Miller, M. S. (1990). Teacher-researcher collaboratives: Cooperative professional development. *Theory into Practice, 24,* 196–202.

Allington, R. L. (1983). The reading instruction provided readers of differing reading abilities. *The Elementary School Journal, 83,* 548–559.

Anderson, T. H., & Armbruster, B. B. (1981). Content area textbooks. *Proceedings of the Conference on Learning to Read in American Schools: Basal Readings and Content Texts,* Tarrytown, NY.

Anderson, R. C., Hiebert, E. H., Scott, J. A., & Wilkinson, I. A. G. (1985). *Becoming a nation of readers.* Washington, DC: U.S. Department of Education, National Institute of Education.

Armbruster, B. B. (1993). Reading to learn: Science and reading. *The Reading Teacher, 46,* 346–347.

Audette, B., & Algozzine, B. (1992). Free and appropriate education for all students: Total quality and the transformation of American public education. *Remedial and Special Education, 13*(6), 8–18.

Baker, L., & Brown, A. (1984). Metacognitive skills and reading. In P. D. Pearson (Ed.), *The handbook of reading research* (pp. 363–364). New York: Longman.

Baldauf, R. B. (1982). The effects of guessing and item dependence on the reliability and validity of recognition based cloze tests. *Educational and Psychological Measurement, 42,* 855–867.

Barnett, D. W., & Macmann, G. M. (1992). Decision reliability and validity: Contributions and limitations of alternative assessment strategies. *The Journal of Special Education, 25,* 431–452.

Bensoussan, M., & Ramraz, R. (1984). Testing EFL reading comprehension using a multiple-choice rational cloze. *The Modern Language Journal, 68,* 230–239.

167

Berk, R. A. (1979). The relative merits of item transformations and the cloze procedure for the measurement of reading comprehension. *The Reading Teacher, 11*, 129–138.

Berliner, D. C. (1985). Effective classroom teaching: The necessary but not sufficient condition for developing exemplary schools. In G. R. Austin, H. Garber (Eds.), *Research on exemplary schools* (pp. 127–154). New York: Academic Press.

Blankenship, C. S. (1985). Using curriculum-based assessment data to make instructional decisions. *Exceptional Children, 52*, 233–238.

Botel, M. (1978). *Botel Reading Inventory.* Chicago: Follet.

Brandt, R. (1993). On outcomes-based education: A conversation with Bill Spady. *Educational Leadership, 50*(4), 66–70.

Bulgren, J. S., Schumaker, J., & Deshler, D. D. (1988). Effectiveness of a concept teaching routine in enhancing the performance of LD students in secondary-level mainstream classes. *Learning Disability Quarterly, 11*(1), 3–17.

Burke, J. C. (1992). *Decreasing classroom behavior problems: Practical guidelines for teachers.* San Diego: Singular Publishing Group.

Carbo, M. (1983). Research in reading and learning style: Implications for exceptional children. *Exceptional Children, 49*, 486–494.

Carbo, M. (1987). Reading style research: "What works" isn't always phonics. *Phi Delta Kappan, 68*, 431–435.

Carnine, D. (1991). Curricular interventions for teaching higher order thinking skills to all students: Introduction to the special series. *Journal of Learning Disabilities, 24*, 261–269.

Carnine, D., Silbert, J., & Kameenui, E. J. (1990). *Direct instruction reading* (2nd ed.). Columbus: Merrill.

Cawley, J. F., Miller, J. H., & Carr, S. C. (1990). An examination of the reading performance of students with mild educational handicaps. *Journal of Learning Disabilities, 23*, 284–290.

Cawley, J. F., & Parmar, R. S. (1992). Arithmetic programming for students with disabilities: An alternative. *Remedial and Special Education, 13*(3), 6–18.

Cawley, J. F., & Parmar, R. S. (1991). Maximizing success in the regular classroom. In G. Stoner, M. R. Shinn, & H. M. Walker (Eds.), *Interventions for achievement and behavior problems* (pp. 415–438), Silver Spring, MD: National Association of School Psychologists.

Chalfant, J. C., & Pysh, M. V. D. (1989). Teacher assistance teams: Five descriptive studies on 96 teams. *Remedial and Special Education, 10*(6), 49–58.

Christenson, S. L., Ysseldyke, J. E., & Thurlow, M. L. (1989). Critical instructional factors for students with mild handicaps: An integrative review. *Remedial and Special Education, 10*(5), 21–31.

Coleman, J. M., & Minnett, A. M. (1993). Learning disabilities and social competence: A social ecological perspective. *Exceptional Children, 59*, 234–246.

Coleman, M., Wheeler, L., & Webber, J. (1993). Research on interpersonal problem-solving training: A review. *Remedial and Special Education, 14*(2), 25–37.

Cone, J. D. (1987). Intervention planning using adaptive behavior instruments. *Journal of Special Education, 21*, 127–148.

Cooke, N. L., Heward, W. L., Test, D. W., Spooner, F., & Courson, F. H. (1991).

Student performance data in the classroom: Measurement and evaluation of student progress. *Teacher Education and Special Education, 14,* 155–161.

Cummings, C. S. (1992). *Using curriculum-based assessment to increase rates of geography skill acquisition in secondary level students with learning disabilities.* Unpublished doctoral dissertation, The Johns Hopkins University, Baltimore.

Database. (1992, May 18). *U.S. News and World Report.* pp. 12.

de Blij, H. J., Danzer, G. A., Hart, R. A., & Drummond, D. W. (1989). *World geography.* Glenview, IL: Scott, Foresman.

De Haas-Warner, S. J. (1991). Effects of self-monitoring on preschoolers' on-task behavior: A pilot study. *Topics in Early Childhood Special Education, 11*(2), 59–73.

Delquadri, J., Greenwood, C. R., Whorton, D., Carta, J. J., & Hall, R. V. (1986). Classwide peer tutoring. *Exceptional Children, 52,* 535–542.

Deno, S. L. (1985). Curriculum-based measurement: The emerging alternative. *Exceptional Children, 52,* 219–232.

Deno, S. (1986). Formative evaluation of individual programs; A new role for school psychologists. *School Psychology Review, 15,* 358–374.

Deno, S. L., & Fuchs, L. S. (1987). Developing curriculum-based measurement systems for data-based special education problem solving. *Focus on Exceptional Children, 19,* 1–16.

Deno, S. L., Mirkin, P. K., & Chiang, B. (1982). Identifying valid measures of reading. *Exceptional Children, 49,* 36–45.

DeSanti, R. J., & Sullivan, V. G. (1984). Inter-rater reliability of the cloze reading inventory as a qualitative measure of reading comprehension. *Reading Psychology: An International Quarterly, 5,* 203–208.

Deshler, D. D. (1978). Psychoeducational aspects of learning disabled adolescents. In L. Mann, L. Goodman, & J. L. Wiederholt (Eds.), *Teaching the learning disabled adolescent.* Boston: Houghton Mifflin.

Deshler, D., & Graham, S. (1980). Tape recording educational materials for secondary handicapped students. *Teaching Exceptional Children, 12,* 52–54.

Deshler, D. D., & Schumaker, J. B. (1986). Learning strategies: An instructional alternative for low-achieving students. *Exceptional Children, 52,* 583–590.

Deshler, D. D., Schumaker, J. B., Lenz, K., & Ellis, E. (1984). Academic and cognitive interventions for LD adolescents: Part II. *Journal of Learning Disabilities, 17,* 170–179.

Diez, M. E., & Moon, C. J. (1992). What do we want students to know? . . . and other important questions. *Educational Leadership, 49*(8), 38–41.

Dolch, E. (1950). *Dolch Word List.* Morristown, NJ: General Learning.

Donahoe, K., & Zigmond, N. (1990). Academic grades of ninth-grade urban learning-disabled students and low-achieving peers. *Exceptionality, 1,* 17–27.

Doyle, W. (1983). Academic work. *Review of Educational Research, 53,* 159–200.

Durkin, D. (1978). What classroom observations reveal about reading comprehension instruction. *Reading Research Quarterly, 14,* 481–533.

Ellis, E. S., & Lenz, B. K. (1987). A component analysis of effective learning strategies for LD students. *Learning Disabilities Focus, 2,* 94–107.

Ellis, E. S., Lenz, B. K., & Sabornie, E. J. (1987). Generalization and adaptation of learning strategies to natural environments: Part 2: Research into practice. *Remedial and Special Education, 8*(2), 6–23.

Elksnin, L. K. (1989). Teaching mildly handicapped students social skills in secondary settings. *Academic Therapy, 25,* 153–169.

Ekwall, E. (1981). *Locating and correcting reading difficulties* (3rd ed.). Columbus, OH: Merrill.

Englert, C. S. (1984). Effective direct instruction practices in special education settings. *Remedial and Special Education, 5*(2), 38–47.

Englert, C. S., Tarrant, K. L., & Mariage, T. V. (1992). Defining and redefining instructional practice in special education: Perspectives on good teaching. *Teacher Education and Special Education, 15,* 62–86.

Epstein, M. H., & Cullinan, D. (1987). Effective social skills curricula for behaviorally disordered students. *The Pointer, 31*(2), 21–24.

Evans, I. M. (1985). Building systems models as a strategy for target behavior selection in clinical assessment. *Behavioral Assessment, 7,* 21–32.

Fad, K. S., & Ryser, G. R. (1993). Social/behavioral variables related to success in general education. *Remedial and Special Education, 14*(1), 25–35.

Farr, R. C. (1969). *Reading: What can be measured?* Newark, DE: International Reading Association Research Fund.

Flood, J. (1986). The text, the student, and the teacher: Learning from exposition in the middle schools. *The Reading Teacher, 39,* 784–791.

Foley, R. M., & Epstein, M. H. (1993). A structured instructional system for developing the school survival skills of adolescents with behavioral disorders. *Behavioral Disorders, 18,* 139–147.

Franklin, M. E. (1992). Culturally sensitive instructional practices for African-American learners with disabilities. *Exceptional Children, 59,* 115–122.

Frazier, D. M., & Paulson, F. L. (1992). How portfolios motivate reluctant writers. *Educational Leadership, 49*(8), 62–65.

Fuchs, L. S., Butterworth, J. R., & Fuchs, D. (1989). Effects of ongoing curriculum-based measurement on student awareness of goals and progress. *Education and Treatment of Children, 12,* 63–72.

Fuchs, L. S., & Deno, S. L. (1991). Paradigmatic distinctions between instructionally relevant measurement models. *Exceptional Children, 58,* 488–500.

Fuchs, L. S., & Deno, S. L. (1992). Effects of curriculum within curriculum-based measurement. *Exceptional Children, 59,* 232–243.

Fuchs, L. S., Deno, S. L., & Mirkin, P. K. (1984). Effects of frequent curriculum-based measurement of evaluation on pedagogy, student achievement, and student awareness of learning. *American Educational Research Journal, 21,* 449–460.

Fuchs, L. S., & Fuchs, D. (1985). Effectiveness of systematic formative evaluation: A meta analysis. *Exceptional Children, 53,* 199–208.

Fuchs, L. S., & Fuchs, D. (1986). Curriculum-based assessment of progress toward long-term and short-term goals. *The Journal of Special Education, 20,* 69–81.

Fuchs, L. S., Fuchs, D., & Bishop, N. (1992). Teacher planning for students with learning disabilities: Differences between general and special educators. *Learning Disabilities Research & Practice, 7,* 120–128.

Fuchs, L. S., Fuchs, D., & Hamlett, C. L. (1992). Computer applications to facilitate curriculum-based measurement. *Teaching Exceptional Children, 24*(4), 58–60.

Fuchs, L. S., Fuchs, D., Hamlett, C. L., & Allinder, R. M. (1991a). The contribution of skills analysis to curriculum-based measurement in spelling. *Exceptional Children, 57,* 443–452.

Fuchs, L. S., Fuchs, D., Hamlett, C. L., & Allinder, R. M. (1991b). Effects of expert system advice within curriculum-based measurement on teacher planning and student achievement in spelling. *School Psychology Review, 20,* 49–66.

Fuchs, L. S., Fuchs, D., Hamlett, C. L., & Stecker, P. M. (1990). The role of skills analysis in curriculum-based measurement in math. *School Psychology Review, 19,* 6–22.

Fuchs, L., Fuchs, D., & Maxwell, L. (1988). The validity of informal reading comprehension measures. *Remedial and Special Education, 9,* 20–28.

Fuchs, L. S., & Shinn, M. R. (1989). Writing CBM, IEP objectives. In M. Shinn (Ed.), *Curriculum-based measurement: Assessing special children* (pp. 130–152). New York: The Guilford Press.

Gaffney, J., & McCloone, B. (1984, March). *Prior knowledge assessment procedures.* Workshop module presented at the Arizona Council for Exceptional Children, Tucson.

Galagan, J. E. (1985). Psychoeducational testing: Turn out the lights, the party's over. *Exceptional Children, 52,* 288–299.

Gardner, E. F., Rudman, H. C., Karlsen, B., & Merwin, J. C. (1982). *Stanford Achievement Test* (7th ed.). San Antonio: The Psychological Corporation.

Germann, G., & Tindal, G. (1985). An application of curriculum-based assessment: The use of direct and repeated measurement. *Exceptional Children, 52,* 244–265.

Gersten, R., Woodward, J., & Darch, C. (1986). Direct instruction: A research-based approach to curriculum design and teaching. *Exceptional Children, 53,* 17–31.

Giek, K. A. (1992). Monitoring student progress through efficient record keeping. *Teaching Exceptional Children, 24*(3), 22–26.

Graham, S. (1992). Issues in handwriting instruction. *Focus on Exceptional Children, 25*(2), 1–14.

Graham, S., Harris, K. R., & Reid, R. (1992). Developing self-regulated learners. *Focus on Exceptional Children, 24*(6), 1–16.

Gresham, F. M. (1984). Social skills and self-efficacy for exceptional children. *Exceptional Children, 51,* 253–261.

Hansen, C. (1978). Story retelling used with average and learning disabled readers as a measure of reading comprehension. *Learning Disability Quarterly, 1,* 65.

Haring, N. G., & Liberty, K. A. (1990). Matching strategies with performance in facilitating generalization. *Focus on Exceptional Children, 22*(8), 1–16.

Harper, R. A., & Stoltman, J. P. (1989). *World geography.* New York: Scholastic.

Harris, K. R., & Pressley, M. (1991). The nature of cognitive strategy instruction: Interactive strategy construction. *Exceptional Children, 57,* 392–404.

Hasbrouck, J. E., & Tindal, G. (1992). Curriculum-based oral reading fluency norms for students in grades 2 through 5. *Teaching Exceptional Children, 24,* 41–43.

Herman, J. L. (1992). What research tells us about good assessment. *Educational Leadership, 49*(8), 74–78.

Hieronymus, A. N., Hoover, H. D., & Lindquist, E. (1986). *Iowa Test of Basic Skills.* Chicago: The Riverside Publishing Company.

Horton, S. V., & Lovitt, T. C. (1989). Using study guides with three classifications of secondary students. *Journal of Special Education, 22,* 447–462.

Horton, S. V., Lovitt, T. C., & White, O. R. (1992). Teaching mathematics to adolescents classified as educable mentally handicapped: Using calculators to remove the computational onus. *Remedial and Special Education, 13*(3), 36–60.

Howard County Public School System. (1991). *World geography curriculum.* Ellicott City, MD: Howard County.

Howell, K. W., & Morehead, M. K. (1987). *Curriculum-based evaluation for special and remedial education.* Columbus, OH: Merrill.

Hughes, C. A., & Boyle, J. R. (1991). Effects of self-monitoring for on-task behavior and task productivity on elementary students with moderate mental retardation. *Education and Treatment of Children, 14,* 96–111.

Hundert, J., & Houghton, A. (1992). Promoting social interaction of children with disabilities in integrated preschools: A failure to generalize. *Exceptional Children, 58,* 311–320.

Idol, L. (1989). The resource/consulting teacher: An integrated model of service delivery. *Remedial and Special Education, 10*(6), 38–48.

Idol, L., Nevin, A., & Paolucci-Whitcomb, P. (1986). *Models of curriculum-based assessment.* Rockville, MD: Aspen.

Jenkins, J. R., & Jenkins, L. M. (1987). Making peer tutoring work. *Educational Leadership, 44,* 64–68.

Jenkins, J. R., & Leicester, N. (1992). Specialized instruction within general education: A case study of one elementary school. *Exceptional Children, 58,* 555–563.

Johnson, D. D., Levin, K. M., & Pittleman, S. D. (1984). *A field assessment of vocabulary instruction in the elementary classroom* (Program Rep. No. 843). Madison: University of Wisconsin, Wisconsin Center for Education Research.

Juvonen, J., & Bear, G. (1992). Social adjustment of children with and without learning disabilities in integrated classrooms. *Journal of Educational Psychology, 84,* 322–330.

Kaminsky, R. (1989). Evaluating solutions: Monitoring student progress. In M. Shinn & W. D. Tilly III (Eds.), *CBA summer institute 1989* (pp. 474–548). Eugene: University of Oregon.

Kinder, D., & Bursuck, W. (1991). The search for a unified social studies curriculum: Does history really repeat itself? *Journal of Learning Disabilities, 24,* 270–275.

King-Sears, M. E., Richardson, M., & Ray, R. M. (1992). Generalizing curriculum-based measurement from university coursework to school-based practice: Train and hope? *LD Forum, 17*(3), 25–28.

Kintsch, W. (1974). *The representation of meaning in memory*. Hillsdale, NJ: Lawrence Erlbaum.

Knutson, N., & Shinn, M. R. (1991). Curriculum-based measurement: Conceptual underpinnings and integration into problem-solving assessment. *Journal of School Psychology, 29*, 371–393.

LaBerge, D., & Samuels, S. J. (1974). Toward a theory of automatic information processing in reading. *Cognitive Psychology, 6*, 293–323.

Lerner, J. (1985). *Learning disabilities: Theories, diagnosis, and teaching strategies* (4th ed.). Boston: Houghton Mifflin.

Lieberman, A. (1986). Collaborative research: Working with, not working on. *Educational Leadership, 43*(5), 28–32.

Lindsley, O. R. (1990). Precision teaching: By teachers for children. *Teaching Exceptional Children, 22*(3), 10–15.

Lovitt, T. C. (1989). *Introduction to learning disabilities*. Boston: Allyn & Bacon.

Lovitt, T. C., & Horton, S. V. (1991). Adapting textbooks for mildly handicapped adolescents. In G. Stoner, M. R. Shinn, & A. M. Walker (Eds.), *Interventions for achievement and behavior*, Silver Spring, MD: National Association of School Psychologists.

MacArthur, C. A., Schwartz, S. S., & Graham, S. (1991). Effects of a reciprocal peer revision strategy in special education classrooms. *Learning Disabilities Research & Practice, 6*, 201–210.

Mager, R. F. (1972). *Goal analysis*. Belmont, CA: Fearon.

Marston, D. B. (1989). A curriculum-based measurement approach to assessing academic performance: What is it and why do it. In M. R. Shinn (Ed.), *Curriculum-based measurement: Assessing special children* (pp. 18–78). New York: Guilford.

Marston, D. B., & Magnusson, D. (1985). Implementing curriculum-based measurement in regular and special education settings. *Exceptional Children, 52*, 266–276.

Mastropieri, M. A., & Scruggs, T. E. (1988). Increasing content area learning of learning disabled students: Research implementation. *Learning Disabilities Research, 4*, 17–25.

Mastropieri, M. A., & Scruggs, T. E. (1989a). Reconstructive elaborations: Strategies that facilitate content learning. *Learning Disabilities Focus, 4*, 73–77.

Mastropieri, M. A., & Scruggs, T. E. (1989b). Mnemonic social studies instruction: Classroom applications. *Remedial and Special Education, 10*, 40–46.

Mastropieri, M. A., & Scruggs, T. E. (1992). Science for students with disabilities. *Review of Educational Research, 62*, 377–411.

Mastropieri, M. A., Scruggs, T. E., & Levin, J. R. (1986). Direct vs. mnemonic instruction: Relative benefits for exceptional learners. *The Journal of Special Education, 20*, 299–307.

Mastropieri, M. A., Scruggs, T. E., & Shiah, S. (1991). Mathematics instruction for learning disabled students: A review of research. *Learning Disabilities Research & Practice, 6*, 89–98.

Mathur, S. R., & Rutherford, R. B. (1991). Peer-mediated interventions promoting social skills of children and youth with behavioral disorders. *Education and Treatment of Children, 14*, 227–242.

Mayer, R. E. (1989). Models for understanding. *Review of Educational Research, 59*, 43–64.

McAllister, J. R. (1991). Curriculum-based behavioral interventions for preschool children with handicaps. *Topics in Early Childhood Special Education, 11*(2), 48–58.

McGinnis, E., & Goldstein, A. (1984). *Skillstreaming the elementary school child: A guide for teaching prosocial skills.* Champaign, IL: Research Press.

Mehring, T. A., & Colson, S. E. (1990). Motivation and mildly handicapped learners. *Focus on Exceptional Children, 22*(5), 1–14.

Mercer, C. D., King-Sears, P., & Mercer, A. R. (1990). States' definitions of learning disabilities. *Journal of Learning Disabilities, 13*, 141–152.

Mercer, C., & Mercer, A. (1985). *Teaching students with learning problems* (2nd ed.). Columbus, OH: Merrill.

Mercer, C. D., & Miller, S. P. (1992). Teaching students with learning problems in math to acquire, understand, and apply basic math facts. *Remedial and Special Education, 13*(3), 19–35.

Meyer, C. A. (1992). What's the difference between authentic and performance assessment? *Educational Leadership, 49*(8), 39–40.

Miller, R., & McDaniel, E. A. (1989). Enhancing teacher efficacy in special education through the assessment of student performance. *Academic Therapy, 25*, 171–181.

Mirkin, P. K., Deno, S. L., Tindal, G., & Kuehnle, K. (1982). Frequency of measurement and data utilization as factors in standardized behavioral assessment of academic skill. *Journal of Behavioral Assessment, 4*, 361–370.

Montague, M., Bos, C., & Doucette, M. (1991). Affective, cognitive, and metacognitive attributes of eighth-grade mathematical problem solvers. *Learning Disabilities Research & Practice, 6*, 145–151.

Montague, M., Graves, A., & Leavell, A. (1991). Planning, procedural facilitation, and narrative composition of junior high students with learning disabilities. *Learning Disabilities Research & Practice, 6*, 219–224.

Moore, L. J., & Carnine, D. (1989). Evaluating curriculum design in the context of active teaching. *Remedial and Special Education, 10*(4), 28–37.

Myles, B. S., & Simpson, R. L. (1989). Regular educators' modification preferences for mainstreaming mildly handicapped children. *Journal of Special Education, 22*, 479–491.

Myles, B. S., & Simpson, R.L. (1992). General educators' mainstreaming preferences that facilitate acceptance of students with behavioral disorders and learning disabilities. *Behavioral Disorders, 17*, 305–315.

National Council of Teachers of Mathematics. (1989). *Curriculum evaluation standards for school mathematics.* Reston, VA: Author.

Nolet, V., & Tindal, G. (1993). Special education in content area classes: Development of a model and practical procedures. *Remedial and Special Education, 14*(1), 36–48.

Notari, A. R., & Drinkwater, S. G. (1991). Best practices for writing child outcomes: An evaluation of two methods. *Topics in Early Childhood Special Education, 11*(3), 92–106.

O'Neil, J. (1992). Putting performance assessment to the test. *Educational Leadership, 49*(8), 14–19.

O'Neill, R. E., Horner, R. H., Albin, R. W., Storey, K., & Sprague, J. R. (1990). *Functional analysis of problem behavior: A practical assessment guide.* Sycamore, IL: Sycamore.

Orasanu, J., & Penney, M. (1986). Introduction: Comprehension theory and how it grew. In *Reading comprehension: From research to practice*, J. Orasanu (Ed.), Hillsdale, NJ: Lawrence Erlbaum.

Ortiz, A. A., & Wilkinson, C. Y. (1992). Assessment and intervention model for the bilingual exceptional student. *Teacher Education and Special Education, 14*, 35–42.

Osborn, J. (1984). The purpose, uses, and contents of workbooks and some guidelines for teachers and publishers. In R. C. Anderson, J. Osborn, & R. J. Tierney (Eds.), *Learning to read in American Schools: Basal readers and content texts* (pp. 45–111). Hillsdale, NJ: Erlbaum.

Paris, S. J., Oka, E. R., & Debritto, A. M. (1983). Beyond decoding: Synthesis of research on reading comprehension. *Educational Leadership, 41*.

Parmar, R. S., & Cawley, J. F. (1991). Challenging the routines and passivity that characterize arithmetic instruction for children with mild handicaps. *Remedial and Special Education, 12*(5), 23–32.

Pearson, P. D. (1985). Changing the face of reading comprehension instruction. *The Reading Teacher, 38*, 724–738.

Peckham, P. D., & Roe, M. D. (1977). The effects of frequent testing. *Journal of Research and Development in Education, 10*(3), 40–50.

Pikulski, J. J., & Pikulski, E. C. (1977). Cloze, maze, and teacher judgment. *The Reading Teacher, 30*, 776–780.

Potter, M. L., & Wamre, H. M. (1990). Curriculum-based measurement and developmental reading models: Opportunities for cross-validation. *Exceptional Children, 57*, 16–25.

Pray, B. S. Jr., Hall, C. W., & Markley, R. P. (1992). Social skills training: An analysis of social behaviors selected for Individualized Education Programs. *Remedial and Special Education, 13*(5), 43–49.

Prater, M. A., Hogan, S., & Miller, S. R. (1992). Using self-monitoring to improve on-task behavior and academic skills of an adolescent with mild handicaps across special and regular education settings. *Education and Treatment of Children, 15*, 43–55.

Putnam, M. L. (1992). The testing practices of mainstream secondary classroom teachers. *Remedial and Special Education, 13*(5), 11–21.

Pyrczak, F. (1976). Context-independence of items designed to measure the ability to derive the meanings of words from their context. *Educational and Psychological Measurement, 36*, 919–924.

Rasool, J. M., & Royer, J. M. (1986). Assessment of reading comprehension using the sentence verification technique: Evidence from narrative and descriptive texts. *Journal of Educational Research, 79*, 180–184.

Ravitch, D., & Finn, C. E. (1987). *What do our 17-year-olds know?* New York: Harper & Row.

Reiher, T. C. (1992). Identified deficits and their congruence to the IEP for behaviorally disordered students. *Behavioral Disorders, 17*, 167–177.

Reschly, D. J. (1992). Special education decision making and functional/behavioral assessment. In W. Stainback & S. Stainback (Eds.), *Controver-*

sial issues confronting special education (pp. 127–138). Boston: Allyn & Bacon.

Rosenshine, B., & Meister, C. (1992). The use of scaffolds for teaching higher-level cognitive strategies. *Educational Leadership, 8,* 26–33.

Royer, J. M., & Cunningham, D. J. (1981). On the theory and measurement of reading comprehension. *Contemporary Educational Psychology, 6,* 187–216.

Royer, J., Hastings, C., & Hook, C. (1979). A sentence verification technique for measuring reading comprehension. *Journal of Reading Behavior, 11,* 355–363.

Royer, J. M., Lynch, D. J., Hambleton, R. K., & Bulgareli, C. (1984). Using the sentence verification technique to assess the comprehension of technical text as a function of subject matter expertise. *American Educational Research Journal, 21,* 839–869.

Rutherford, F. J., & Ahlgren, A. (1990). *Science for all Americans.* New York: Oxford Press.

Sager, R. J., Helgren, D. M., & Israel, S. (1992). *World geography today.* Austin, TX: Harcourt, Brace, Jovanovich.

Salend, S. J., & Meddaugh, D. (1985). Using a peer-mediated extinction procedure to decrease obscene language. *The Pointer, 30,* 8–11.

Salvia, J., & Hughes, C. (1990). *Curriculum-based assessment: Testing what is taught.* New York: Macmillan.

Salvia, J., & Ysseldyke, J. (1991). *Assessment* (5th ed.). Boston: Houghton Mifflin.

Samuels, S. J. (1976). Modes of word recognition. In H. Singer & R. B. Ruddell (Eds), *Theoretical models and processes of reading* (pp. 68–82). Newark, DE: International Reading Association.

Sawyer, R. J., Graham, S., & Harris, K. R. (1992). Direct teaching, strategy instruction, and strategy instruction with explicit self-regulation: Effects on the composition skills and self-efficacy of students with learning disabilities. *Journal of Educational Psychology, 84,* 340–352.

Schultz, J. B., Carpenter, C. D., & Turnbull, A. P. (1991). *Mainstreaming exceptional students* (3rd ed.). Boston: Allyn & Bacon.

Schumaker, J. B., Denton, P. H., & Deshler, D. D. (1984). *Learning strategies curriculum: The paraphrasing strategy.* Lawrence, KS: University of Kansas.

Scruggs, T. E., & Mastropieri, M. A. (1993). Current approaches to science education: Implications for mainstream instruction of students with learning disabilities. *Remedial and Special Education, 14*(1), 15–24.

Scruggs, T. E., & Richter, L. (1988). Tutoring learning disabled students: A critical review. *Learning Disabilities Quarterly, 11,* 274–286.

Shavelson, R. J., & Baxter, G. P. (1992). What we've learned about assessing hands-on science. *Educational Leadership, 49*(8), 20–25.

Shinn, M. R. (1988). Development of curriculum-based local norms for use in special education decision-making. *School Psychology Review, 17,* 61–80.

Shinn, M. R., & Hubbard, D. D. (1992). Curriculum-based measurement and problem-solving assessment: Basic procedures and outcomes. *Focus on Exceptional Children, 24*(5), 1–20.

Shinn, M. R., Rosenfield, S., & Knutson, N. (1989). Curriculum-based assessment: A comparison of models. *School Psychology Review, 18,* 299–316.

Silvaroli, N. J. (1973). *Classroom Reading Inventory* (2nd ed.). Dubuque, IA: William C. Brown.

Simpson, R. L., Whelan, R. J., & Zabel, R. H. (1993). Special education personnel preparation in the 21st century: Issues and strategies. *Remedial and Special Education, 14*(2), 7–22.

Singer, H. (1978). Active comprehension: From answering to asking questions. *The Reading Teacher,* 901–906.

Slavin, R. E., & Madden, N. A. (1989). What works for students at-risk: A research synthesis. *Educational Leadership, 46*(5), 4–13.

Spache, G. D. (1972). *Diagnostic Reading Scales.* Monterey, CA: CTB/McGraw-Hill.

Spiro, R. J., Bruce, B. C., & Brewer, W. F. (1980). Introduction to global issues. In R. J. Spiro, B. C. Bruce, & W. F. Brewer (Eds.), *Theoretical issues in reading comprehension* (pp. 1–17), Hillsdale, NJ: Lawrence Erlbaum.

Stainback, S., & Stainback, W. (1992). Schools as inclusive communities. In W. Stainback & S. Stainback (Eds.), *Controversial issues confronting special education* (pp. 29–44). Boston: Allyn & Bacon.

Starlin, C., & Starlin, A. (1974). *Guidelines for continuous decision-making.* Bemedji, MN: Unique Curriculums Unlimited.

Stokes, T. F., & Osnes, P. G. (1986). Programming the generalization of children's social behavior. In P. S. Strain, M. J. Guralnick, & H. M. Walker (Eds.), *Children's social behavior* (pp. 407–439). Orlando: Academic Press.

Swanson, H. L. (1987). *Memory and learning disabilities: Advances in learning and behavior disabilities.* Greenwich, CT: JAI Press.

Szetela, W., & Nicol, D. (1992). Evaluating problem solving in mathematics. *Educational Leadership, 49*(8), 42–45.

Thorndike, R., & Hagen, E. (1978). *Measurement and evaluation in psychology in education.* New York: Wiley.

Tierney, R. J., Carter, M. A., & Desai, L. E. (1991). *Portfolio assessment in the reading-writing classroom.* Norwood, MA: Christopher-Gordon.

Tindal, G. A., & Marston, D. B. (1990). *Classroom-based assessment.* New York: Macmillan.

Tindal, G., & Parker, R. (1991). Identifying measures for evaluating written expression. *Learning Disabilities Research & Practice, 6,* 211–218.

Tucker, J. A. (1985). Curriculum-based assessment: An introduction. *Exceptional Children, 52,* 199–204.

U.S. House of Representatives, *Elementary and secondary conference report to accompany H.R. 5* (Report 100-526, April 13, 1988, p. 85).

Van Reusen, A. K., & Bos, C. (1990). I PLAN: Helping students communicate in planning conferences. *Teaching Exceptional Children, 22*(4), 30–32.

Vergason, G. A., & Anderegg, M. L. (1991). Beyond the Regular Education Initiative and the resource room controversy. *Focus on Exceptional Children, 23*(7), 1–6.

Walley, C. (1993). An invitation to reading fluency. *The Reading Teacher, 46,* 526–527.

Walther, M., & Beare, P. (1991). The effect of videotape feedback on the on-task behavior of a student with emotional/behavioral disorders. *Education and Treatment of Children, 14,* 53–60.

Wang, M. C., Walberg, H., & Reynolds, M. C. (1992). A scenario for better — not separate — special education. *Educational Leadership, 50*(2), 35–38.

Waugh, R. P. (1978). *Research for teachers: Teaching students to comprehend.* Portland, OR: Northwest Regional Laboratory.

Weaver, C. (1988). *Reading Process and Practice.* Portsmouth, NH: Heinemann.

Webber, J., Scheuermann, B., McCall, C., & Coleman, M. (1993). Research on self-monitoring as a behavior management technique in special education classrooms: A descriptive review. *Remedial and Special Education, 14*(2), 38–56.

Welch, M. (1992). The PLEASE strategy: A metacognitive learning strategy for improving the paragraph writing of students with mild learning disabilities. *Learning Disability Quarterly, 15*, 119–128.

Wesson, C., Otis-Wilborn, A., Hasbrouck, J., & Tindal, G. (1989). Linking assessment, curriculum, and instruction of oral and written language. *Focus on Exceptional Children, 22*(4), 1–12.

Wesson, C. L., Vierthaler, J. M., & Haubrich, P. A. (1989). An efficient technique for establishing reading groups. *The Reading Teacher*, 466–469.

West, R. P., & Young, K. R. (Eds.). (1990). Precision teaching [Special issue]. *Teaching Exceptional Children, 22*(3).

Whinnery, K. W., & Fuchs, L. S. (1992). Implementing effective teaching strategies with learning disabled students through curriculum-based measurement. *Learning Disabilities Research and Practice, 7*, 25–30.

Wiggins, G. (1989). The futility of trying to teach everything of importance. *Educational Leadership, 47*(3), 23–40.

Wiggins, G. (1992). Creating tests worth taking. *Educational Leadership, 49*(8), 26–33.

Wilson, M. (1988). How can we teach reading in the content areas? In C. Weaver, *Reading process and practice.* Portsmouth, NH: Heinemann Educational Books.

Wolf, D. P., LeMahieu, P. G., & Eresh, J. (1992). Good measure: Assessment as a tool for educational reform. *Educational Leadership, 49*(8), 8–13.

Woodcock, R. M., & Johnson, M. B. (1989). *Woodcock-Johnson Psychoeducational Battery — Revised.* Hingham, MA: Teaching Resources.

Woodward, J., & Noell, J. (1991). Science instruction at the secondary level: Implications for students with learning disabilities. *Journal of Learning Disabilities, 24*, 277–284.

World geography curriculum guide. (1991). Ellicott City, MD: Howard County Public School System.

Young, L. E. (1992). Critical thinking skills: Definitions, implications for implementation. *NASSP Bulletin, 76*, 47–54.

Ysseldyke, J. (1983). Current practices in making psychoeducational decisions about learning disabled students. *Journal of Learning Disabilities, 16*, 226–233.

Zaragoza, N., & Vaughn, S. (1992). The effects of process writing instruction on three 2nd-grade students with different achievement profiles. *Learning Disabilities Research & Practice, 7*, 128–193.

Zigmond, N., Vallecorsa, A., & Reinhardt, G. (1980). Reading instruction for students with learning disabilities. *Topics in Language Disorders, 1*, 89–98.

GLOSSARY

auditory discrimination — the ability to accurately distinguish one sound or combination of sounds from another when presented with aural stimuli (sound)

auditory memory — the ability to accurately remember a sound or group of sounds after aural presentation to use the information to decode or encode words

authentic assessment — an assessment in which the student demonstrates the desired behavior in a real-life context

basal reading series — a commercially produced series of reading books and materials generally including scope and sequence charts of skills to be introduced, taught, and practiced

blending — the act of sequentially combining individual sounds within a word to form the complete word

cloze — a task that assesses reading comprehension, with the student supplying words that have been systematically deleted from a text

cognition — the act or process of thinking and using acquired knowledge

comprehension — gaining information from what one has read

critical comprehension — the use of information one has read to evaluate or make judgments

criterion-referenced test — test comparing individual performance to a predetermined mastery level

curriculum-based assessment (CBA) — the ongoing process of testing students based upon skills that have been or are being taught within the student's school curriculum; any set of measurement procedures employing direct and frequent observation and recording of student performance in the local curriculum and are used to make instructional decisions

curriculum-based measurement (CBM) — direct and frequent measure of a student's progress and performance within the school curriculum that encompasses long-term goals

curriculum-based system — an organized approach to assessment in which students are assessed within the context of their school curriculum — with assessments short and ongoing, data recorded, and decisions about instruction made based on the data

decoding — the breaking apart of words into sounds or combinations of sounds and then blending to form whole words

formative evaluation — ongoing student progress assessment, using the results of the assessments to make instructional decisions

functional words — those sight words needed for one to effectively function within society

graded word lists — words identified as readable by most average students at a given grade level

Individualized Education Plan (IEP) — document mandated by federal law for all students with disabilities that outlines short- and long-term objectives for their special education programming

inferential comprehension — the use of information one has read drawing conclusions about that information

least restrictive environment (LRE) — the school environment with the fewest special education supports within which a student with disabilities can learn and be successful

literal comprehension — the recognition, location, or recall of information specifically presented

maze — a task assessing reading comprehension that has the student supply words systematically deleted from the text and providing a number of choices for each blank

norm-referenced tests — tests comparing individual performance to peer performance

oral reading fluency — the combination of accuracy and reading rate in evaluating success in reading words within text

paraphrasing — a test of comprehension in which the student is asked to retell a story in the youngster's own words

performance assessment — an evaluation requiring the student to complete or demonstrate behavior the assessor desires to measure

phonics — a system of teaching reading in which students are taught basic letter-sound correspondences in conjunction with rules for "sounding out" or "decoding" unknown words

portfolio assessment — the systematic collection of ongoing student work by both students and teachers

production-type responses — responses to test items in which the student is required to perform the behavior of concern, usually by reading aloud, writing, or speaking

reading rate — the speed with which one reads words within context, usually in combination with accuracy

retelling — a test of comprehension in which the student is asked to tell everything remembered from a text

school survival skills — basic skills required for success in most classrooms, such as turning in work on time, following directions

selection-type responses — responses to test items in which the student is not required to perform the behavior of concern; rather the student is able to select from formats such as matching, multiple choice, or crossing out correct or incorrect items

sight words vocabulary — words that one can read automatically without the aid of phonetic rules or context clues, usually within 1 second

social skills — verbal and nonverbal communication skills required to get along with others, resolve disputes, accept criticism, and so forth

sound/symbol relationships — the sounds associated with individual or groups of letters

strategic readers — readers who employ specific techniques to aid in remembering what has been read

summative evaluation — assessing student progress on completion of instruction

visual discrimination — the ability to accurately distinguish one visual stimuli from another

visual memory — the ability to accurately remember visual stimuli after presentation

whole language — an approach to teaching reading in which the importance of the language and experiences of the child are emphasized as a basis for reading and writing

word recognition — the automatic reading of words without the aid of phonetic rules or context clues

APPENDIX A

■

SAMPLE PROBES AND DATA COLLECTION SHEETS FOR CBA

Reading Comprehension Assessment
Curriculum-based Assessment
Data Sheet

Student:	Date:
Pages read:	
Score for comprehension statement	
Code: 3 = excellent 2 = fair	1 = poor

Student:	Date:
Pages read:	
Score for comprehension statement	
Code: 3 = excellent 2 = fair	1 = poor

Student:	Date:
Pages read:	
Score for comprehension statement	
Code: 3 = excellent 2 = fair	1 = poor

Student:	Date:
Pages read:	
Score for comprehension statement	
Code: 3 = excellent 2 = fair	1 = poor

Materials needed:
1.   Textbook (which may be from any content area) for student to read from;
2.   Questions about the passage the student has read;
3.   Timer (if the amount of time to read is to be controlled);
4.   Graph (labeled 1-3) to indicate score for comprehension statement.

Reading Fluency Assessment
Curriculum-based Assessment
Data Sheet

Student: Date:
Number of words in passage:
Passage level:
Number of errors:
Percentage of words correctly read:

Student: Date:
Number of words in passage:
Passage level:
Number of errors:
Percentage of words correctly read:

Student: Date:
Number of words in passage:
Passage level:
Number of errors:
Percentage of words correctly read:

Student: Date:
Number of words in passage:
Passage level:
Number of errors:
Percentage of words correctly read:

Materials needed:
  1. Textbook (which may be from any content area) for student to
      read from;
  2. Timer (if the amount of time to read is to be controlled);
  3. Graph (labeled 1–100%) to indicate score for fluency
      statement.

Consonant Sounds
Curriculum-based Assessment
Data Sheet

Objective:
> When given 10 flashcards with pictures of familiar objects (object names reviewed with student previously), the student will identify 9 out of 10 initial consonant sounds correctly, 8 out of 10 trials.

Card 1:   Consonant sound assessed _____   Response, if incorrect _____

Card 2:   Consonant sound assessed _____   Response, if incorrect _____

Card 3:   Consonant sound assessed _____   Response, if incorrect _____

Card 4:   Consonant sound assessed _____   Response, if incorrect _____

Card 5:   Consonant sound assessed _____   Response, if incorrect _____

Card 6:   Consonant sound assessed _____   Response, if incorrect _____

Card 7:   Consonant sound assessed _____   Response, if incorrect _____

Card 8:   Consonant sound assessed _____   Response, if incorrect _____

Card 9:   Consonant sound assessed _____   Response, if incorrect _____

Card 10: Consonant sound assessed _____   Response, if incorrect _____

Total amount correct out of 10:

Program modifications, if needed:

Reading
Curriculum-based Assessment
Probe Sheet

Objective:

    Given a passage of approximately fifty words from a familiar Core Book at the 3/1 Level, the student will orally read the words missing in the passage with 80% accuracy, 3 out of 4 opportunities.

Passage selected from <u>Bread and Jam for Frances</u>

    It was breakfast _____ and everyone was sitting at the _____. Father was eating his egg. Mother was eating her _____, too.

    Gloria was sitting in a _____ and eating her _____, too. Frances was eating _____ and jam.

    "What a lovely _____!" said Father. "If there is _____ thing I am fond of for _____, it is a soft-boiled _____."

Student name:

Date given:

Test giver:

_____ correct responses

————————————————————————— X 100 = _____ % correct

    10 possible responses

Special notes here:

Spoken Language
Curriculum-based Assessment
Data Sheet

Objective:

    During class discussions, the student will answer questions with semantically correct sentences (relates to topic and expresses a complete thought) in 4 out of 5 opportunities. The student will maintain this level for 10 consecutive days.

* * *

Question 1
Response:

Semantically correct	yes_____	no_____
Complete sentence	yes_____	no_____

* * *

Question 2
Response:

Semantically correct	yes_____	no_____
Complete sentence	yes_____	no_____

* * *

Question 3
Response:

Semantically correct	yes_____	no_____
Complete sentence	yes_____	no_____

* * *

Question 4
Response:

Semantically correct	yes_____	no_____
Complete sentence	yes_____	no_____

* * *

Question 5
Response:

Semantically correct	yes_____	no_____
Complete sentence	yes_____	no_____

**Written Language
Curriculum-based Assessment
Student Response Sheet (Probe)**

Student name: Date: Probe #

Curriculum: Written composition - Sentence writing

Objective:
     Given a list of nouns and verbs, student will write complete sentences
     using subject/predicate pattern 4 out of 5 times.

       Nouns (Subject)   Verbs (Predicate)
1.
2.
3.
4.
5.

Sentences: Check here if complete:

1.

2.

3.

4.

5.

                                                    Score:
                                              (# complete)

Mastery = 4 complete sentences

Written Language
Curriculum-based Assessment
Probe Sheet

Curriculum: Written composition - Sentence writing

Objective:
Using a class-generated adjective/adverb word list and sentences previously written, the student will expand sentences by using descriptive words with 70% accuracy on a 10 sentence sample.

Directions:

_____   student writes 10 sentences

_____   score student sample by counting the number of complete sentences

_____   look for a descriptor (adjective/adverb) in each complete sentence

_____   a complete sentence with at least one descriptor counts for 10%

_____   compute mastery average (70%) based on 10 complete sentences which contain an adjective and/or adverb = 100%

_____   assess two times per week

Mastery is 70%:
7 complete sentences containing a descriptor (adjective/adverb)

Written Language
Curriculum-based Assessment
Probe Sheet

Sentence Writing

Objective:
> Given a writing topic, the student will write 10 related sentences using complete sentence structure 80% of the time (8 out of 10 sentences are related to the topic and complete) in a weekly writing sample.

Directions:

_____   Choose a writing prompt.

_____   Assign the prompt to a student.

_____   Allow one class period for draft and rewrite.

_____   Allow use of visuals and word lists.

Assessment is to be done weekly.

Mastery level = 80% to 100%

Maintenance Mastery level to attain by June = 100%*

*   student will be able to write 10 complete sentences on a topic in a weekly writing sample

Written Language
Curriculum-based Assessment
Probe Sheet

Writing Topic:

1.   Write at least 10 sentences on this topic.
2.   Write your first draft, check it over, and rewrite below.

# of complete sentences _____

# of related sentences _____

% score _____

Math — Recognizing Numbers on a Calculator
Curriculum-based Assessment
Probe

Student: Teacher: KEY: + = correct response
                                              - = incorrect response

Objective:

    During math class when provided with a calculator with enlarged keys and 10 number flashcards, the student will press the corresponding calculator key with 80% accuracy over 5 consecutive trials.

Dates	0	1	2	3	4	5	6	7	8	9	% correct

Note:

    Instructional modifications will be considered if progress has not reached 40% by 5 probes.

<u>Sample Probes for Science and Social Studies</u>

Sample Probe: One-Celled Organisms

Behavioral Objective: Given nine questions from a unit on one-celled organisms, the student will select the correct answer with 100% accuracy within 2 minutes.

Directions: Circle the correct response.

1. What shape are bacilli bacteria?

   a) rod-like   b) spiral   c) spherical

2. Polio, AIDS, and measles are caused by

   a) bacteria   b) viruses   c) fungi

3. Monderans include:

   a) viruses and bacteria   b) bacteria and cyanobacteria

   c) fungi and bacteria

4. The three main shapes of bacteria are:

   a) rod-like, triangular, and spherical

   b) spherical, rod-like, and spiral

   c) triangular, spiral, and spherical

5. In which conditions can bacteria survive?

   a) extreme temperatures

   b) mild temperatures

   c) very cold temperatures only

6. Plant-like protists are similar to cyanobacteria in that both have:

   a) a nucleus   b) chlorophyll   c) mitochondria

7. The three groups of protists include:

   a) protozoans, slime molds, and plant-like protists

   b) protozoans, fungi, and viruses

   c) slime molds, plant-like protists, and fungi

8. Bacteria obtain energy from:

   a) milk, blood, and animals

   b) blood, water, and soil

   c) milk, blood, and soil

9. What is one property of a nonliving virus?

   a) they infect plants and animals

   b) they can be crystallized and stored in bottles for many years

   c) they become attached to the outside of a cell

Sample Probe Measuring Mastery of Key Vocabulary Using

Selection-Type Format

Behavioral Objective: Given four questions from a life sciences unit
on one-celled organisms, the student will
select the correct answer with 100% accuracy
within 1 minute.

1. Moneran are:

    a) rod-like structures

    b) one-celled organisms with no nucleus

    c) one-celled organisms containing a nucleus

____2. protist   a) monderan important in recycling matter

____3. bacteria   b) whip-like thread used by an organism for

____4. flagellum   movement

                      c) a one-celled organism with a nucleus

Sample Probe Measuring Mastery of Key Vocabulary Using Production-Type Format

Behavioral Objective: Given ten vocabulary words from a life sciences unit on one-celled organisms, the student will write the correct definitions with 100% accuracy within 3 minutes.

Directions: Define each vocabulary word below.

1. bacteria-

2. protist-

3. moneran-

4. flagellum-

5. nucleus-

6. protozoa-

7. cell wall-

8. cell membrane-

9. amoeba-

10. algae-

Sample Probe Measuring Mastery of Key Vocabulary and
Requiring Higher-Order Thinking

Behavioral Objective: Given four questions from a life sciences unit on one-celled organisms, the student will write the correct answers with 100% accuracy within 1 minute.

1. What would happen if saprophytic bacteria were all killed?

2. Explain the differences between cyanobacteria and bacteria.

3. Although bacteria are the cause of many infections and diseases they are necessary organisms. Explain why they are necessary.

4. Which are more complex organisms, moneran or protists? Explain your answer.

Sample Probe: Reading Maps

Behavioral Objective: Given a classroom atlas and six questions
                     from a geography unit on reading maps, the
                     student will write the correct answer with
                     100% accuracy within 3 minutes.

1. Using the map found on page ____ of your atlas, measure the
    distance between Washington DC and Atlanta, GA.

    _____ miles

2. In the map on page ____ of your atlas, what does the color red
    represent?

3. Using the map found on page _____ of your atlas, list the
    countries that border France.

4. Using the map found on page ____ of your atlas, identify the
    average amount of rainfall per year in Algeria.

    _____ inches/year

5. According to the map found on page _____ of your atlas, which
    area of Europe is most densely populated?

6. According to the map found on page ____ of your atlas, which
    mountains are taller, the Appalachains or the Rockies?

Sample Probe: Longitude and Latitude

Behavioral Objective: Given a classroom atlas and six questions from a geography unit on finding latitude and longitude, the student will write the correct answer with 100% accuracy within 3 minutes.

1. Using the map found on page ____ of your atlas, identify the latitude and longitude coordinates of Paris, France.

    Latitude- _____ Longitude- _____

2. Using the map found on page ____ of your atlas, identify the latitude and longitude coordinates of Rome, Italy.

    Latitude- _____ Longitude- _____

3. Which of the two cities above probably has a warmer climate? Why?

4. What city can be found at 33^0N latitude and 44^0E longitude?

    _____

5. What is found at 40^0N latitude and 140^0W longitude?

    _____

6. Identify two cities in Europe that probably have similar climates. Why do they have similar climates?

Daily Probe: Interpreting Information From Maps

Behavioral Objective: Given a classroom atlas and six questions
from a geography unit on interpreting
information from maps, the student will
write the correct answer with 100% accuracy
within 3 minutes.

Study the map <u>Earth's Yearly Rainfall Patterns</u> found on page___
and the map <u>Earth's Natural Vegetation Patterns</u> found on page___.
Now answer the questions below based on information contained on
these two maps.

1. Which continent has more desert lands than any other continent?

2. Which continent gets little or no rainfall ever?

3. What kind of vegetation is found in areas with heavy rainfall
   year round?

4. What kind of vegetation is found in areas with low amounts of
   rainfall?

5. What effect does rainfall seem to have on the Earth's vegetation
   patterns?

6. The newspapers frequently report on the hunger and starvation
   found in many of the North African countries. Using the
   information contained in these maps explain why there is such a
   shortage of food in North Africa.

Daily Probe: Key Vocabulary in World Geography Curriculum

Behavioral Objective: Given ten vocabulary words from the World
Geography curriculum, the student will select
the correct definitions with 100% accuracy
within 2 minutes.

Directions: Match column B to column A.

A	B
____1. culture	a) growth in producing goods through the use of machines
____2. exports	
____3. irrigation	b) weather conditions in an area over a long period of time
____4. continent	
____5. climate	c) a model of the Earth
____6. rural	d) bringing water to land
____7. industrialization	e) one of 7 large land masses on Earth
____8. physical geography	
____9. economic geography	f) the way people live
____10. globe	g) having to do with the countryside
	h) goods sent out of the country
	i) the study of how people use resources to earn a living
	j) study of the Earth's natural features

**School Survival Skills
Curriculum-based Assessment
Data Collection Sheet**

Student: Date:
School: Teacher:

Objective:
     In a group of four students during a cooperative learning activity, the
student will remain with his group for 15 minutes (at the independent
level) for 8 out of 10 trials.

Group Activity	Date	Minutes in Group	Level of Prompt
1.			
2.			
3.			
4.			
5.			
6.			
7.			
8.			
9.			
10.			

Mastery of 8 of 10 trials in the group for 15 minutes at the independent level.

Interventions used:

Total number of times 15 minutes in group:
Most frequently used prompt:
Level of prompts: P (physical)
                 G (gestural)
                 V (verbal)
                 I (independently)

APPENDIX B

■

SAMPLE GRAPHS
FOR CBA

Reading
Curriculum-based Assessment
Graph

Objective:
>   Given a list of 50 frequently used sight words (out of context and found
>   in the first grade reading texts), the student will read aloud 40 out of
>   50 words when presented randomly on flashcards and maintain that
>   level for a 4 week period.

# of sight words read correctly out of 50	50
	45
	40
	35
	30
	25
	20
	15
	10
	5
	0

Dates →

Written Language
Curriculum-based Assessment
Graph

Student name: Date:

Objective:
      Given a list of nouns and verbs, the student will write 4 complete
      sentences (subject & predicate).

# of complete sentences											
6											
5											
4											
3											
2											
1											

Dates →

Mastery = 4 complete sentences

Directions:
1.   Graph score daily (student or teacher can do this)
2.   Time frame target for mastery is 10 days
3.   Student should graph 3 scores of 4 or 5 in a row for maintenance
       mastery.
4.   List instructional interventions and note on graph:
       # 1:
       # 2:

Written Language
Curriculum-based Assessment
Graph

Objective:

Using a class-generated adjective/adverb word list and sentences previously written, the student will expand sentences by using descriptive words with 70% accuracy on a 10 sentence sample.

% of
correct
sentences

| 100 |
| 90 |
| 80 |
| 70 |
| 60 |
| 50 |
| 40 |
| 30 |
| 20 |
| 10 |

Date →

Mastery = 70%

Interventions: # 1:
                   # 2:

Math
Curriculum-based Assessment
Graph

Objective:

Given five math problems with sums no greater than 10, the student will successfully add 4 out of 5 addition problems correctly while using sets and manipulatives. He will maintain that level for a 10-day period.

of
addition
problems
done
correctly

```
5
4
3
2
1
0
```

Dates →

INDEX